WHITETAIL COUNTRY

WHITETAIL COUNTRY

WITH 130 COLOR PHOTOGRAPHS BY

DANIEL J. COX

AND TEXT BY

JOHN J. OZOGA

WILLOW CREEK PRESS

My share of this book, the written seasonal text, is dedicated to my wife, Janice, who has spent nearly as many hours as I huddled in dilapidated blinds, peering through dim light at the ghostly images of fleeting whitetails.

John J. Ozoga

Published by Willow Creek Press, P.O. Box 300, Wautoma, WI 54982

ISBN 0-932558-43-7

LC Catalog Card No.
#88-50138

Printed and bound in the United States of America.

First Edition.

Library of Congress Cataloging-in-Publication Data

Ozoga, John J.
    Whitetail country.

    Bibliography: p.
    1. White-tailed deer.   I. Cox, Daniel J., 1960-
II. Title.
QL737.U55097   1988   599.73'57   88-50138
ISBN 0-932558-43-7

FOREWORD

The concept for this illustrated book was formulated in 1985 when professional wildlife photographer Dan Cox came to our offices at Willow Creek Press carrying a portfolio of white-tailed deer photographs. It took little time for us to recognize that Cox's collection of photos was not the average deer photography used to illustrate sporting magazines. These were superlative images of wild whitetails in a natural environment, and not only photographs of deer in fall, when most wildlife photographers choose to capture the drama of the whitetail's breeding season and rutting, large-antlered bucks on film, but photographs of deer in all seasons of the year, of the various age classes of deer of both sexes, and of deer engaged in a wide variety of behaviors.

It was immediately evident that Cox's portfolio was the core of an illustrated life history of the white-tailed deer. But parts of the photographic phenology were missing, important aspects of the whitetail's existence had to be recorded on film before this book could adequately portray the natural history of this widely recognized but relatively furtive, enigmatic animal.

So it was that Cox retreated to Wisconsin's north woods to begin a photographic odyssey of two years duration. During that time, traveling from his home in Duluth, Minnesota, to his study area in northwestern Wisconsin, he spent countless days and hours in whitetail country in the company of his photographic subjects, shooting roll after roll of film in all types of weather throughout the four seasons.

Later, when Cox edited the more than 5,000 slides he had taken of whitetails, the behavioral patterns of the deer were readily identifiable in his photographs. But explaining the significance of the animals' activities illustrated in *Whitetail Country*—however well they were photographically portrayed and regardless of Dan's extensive and insightful observations of the whitetails' behavior in his study area—needed additional elucidation. To what extent are certain behaviors genetically influenced? How does the physical environment determine deer behavior, and to what extent? How similar are deer behaviors among populations in other parts of the whitetail's range in North America?

To authoritatively explain these phenomena, the editors at Willow Creek Press turned to the scientific community and the writing abilities of John Ozoga. Ozoga is one of this country's preeminent whitetail deer biologists and a man gifted not only with the ability to write professional papers for the scientific community, he is also known for his talents as a writer of popular articles about whitetail deer for educated lay readers.

Here, then, is the marriage of the efforts of these two professionals, an incomparable, illustrated life history of the white-tailed deer. The absolutely stunning photography of Daniel Cox and the absorbing text of John Ozoga will take you, the viewer and reader, on an unequivocally unique and unforgettable trip through *Whitetail Country*.

Chuck Petrie
Editor, Willow Creek Press

ABOUT THE PHOTOGRAPHER

Daniel J. Cox, originally a native of the state of Washington, moved to Minnesota in his early teens. It was, he admits, his exposure to the rugged beauty of the Pacific Northwest as well as wilderness regions of the Upper Midwest that helped influence his decision to channel his creative energies and talent toward a lifetime career as a wildlife and wilderness area photographer.

In this fiercely competitive occupation, Dan has risen to become nationally recognized for his professional ability and artistry. His work has included representation in *Time-Life* publications, *National Geographic, National Wildlife, International Wildlife, Readers Digest, Sierra, Field & Stream,* and *Sports Afield* magazines as well as many other state and regional publications. Many of his photographs have been selected for private collections and have been displayed in the prestigious Nikon House Gallery in New York.

In addition to professional goals they've already attained, and those to which they yet aspire, however, Dan and his wife, Julie, who is also his full-time partner in their stock photography business, share another ambition: They hope to help nurture, through Dan's photography, a better understanding and appreciation of our natural resources. Ultimately, they feel, today's conservation and enlightened management of wild animals and their environments will benefit future generations of Americans.

ACKNOWLEDGEMENTS

Contained in this volume is a selection of photographic work that has involved a significant portion of my life. Most recently I spent two years working on this project on a full-time basis, and five years before that on a part-time basis. The culmination of such a long-term undertaking is extremely rewarding and, as with any complicated, drawn-out endeavor, especially producing a book, there were many people involved who won't get the chance to share the glory of the photographer or writer.

Wildlife photography is more than just shooting photographs of animals and nature scenes, it includes studying wild animals and going to the places they inhabit. In searching for these areas I've met many wonderful people. While shooting photographs in Wisconsin for *Whitetail Country*, I could hardly believe the love rural people of that state have for white-tailed deer. Around their townships and villages, some small communities have even established boundaries within which the discharge of firearms is prohibited. Instituted to protect homes, cabins, and recreational properties, these legally protected areas have become sanctuaries for a variety of wildlife species, and whitetails, in particular, flourish in some of these ersatz "refuges."

Some of the people living in the vicinity of these "protected" whitetail populations and who helped me along the way include Stan and Esther Stevenson, two of the finest people I have ever had the pleasure of meeting. For years they have enjoyed watching whitetails, collected dropped antlers, bottle fed orphaned fawns, and protected the herds from roaming dogs. Without the Stevensons' knowledge and desire to show me the things they've seen, I could never have witnessed all that I have.

The generosity and friendship of Troy Hyde and his beautiful wife, Renee, is greatly appreciated. Together we spent some crazy, wild days exploring parts of Wisconsin I didn't know existed. Their front door was always open to me and a soft bed waiting inside, a welcome relief from the cramped quarters of my camper.

Of course, I owe a special thanks to the people who helped me become the person I am today. Without their support, I could never have turned a beloved hobby into a full-time career. They include my mother and father, who love the outdoors, each in their own way. My dad, with patience and love, shared with me his love for the magnificent West, even when I was no more than a whimpering child, but he instilled in me the desire to be afield. My mother, with patience and understanding, has supported my decisions in whatever paths I've chosen to follow. Ed and Arlene Liebe are also special to me; they allowed me, at a very early age, to be a part of their family's life. In doing so, the special bond between Julie and I was formed, an exceptional bond indeed, for the livelihood of a free-lance wildlife photographer is oftentimes dubious, his very existence sometimes precarious.

Most important is the thanks I owe Julie, my wife. She has known me long before I knew what photography was all about. She is a special lady who understands the long hours required to photograph in the wild, and has been willing to share me with the natural world beyond our log cabin door. For me, as with most professional outdoor photographers, weeks away from home are commonplace, and yet never has there been a complaint from her, the one who suffers most. Without her iron will and loving support, I could never have as full a life as I enjoy today.

Finally, I would like to express my sincere gratitude to an individual who has devoted many years to the study of whitetail behavior and who has contributed the text to this book. Mr. John Ozoga is not only a knowledgeable and dedicated biologist, he also has superb writing skills that allow him to convey the information he has learned in an absorbing, relaxed style for educated lay readers. In-depth studies of any animal can be dry and unexciting when transferred from field notes to book form, but Ozoga's text transforms still photographs into moving images, bringing the reader to the meadows and forests inhabited by deer.

Daniel J. Cox

ABOUT THE AUTHOR

John J. Ozoga, a native of Crystal Falls, Michigan, has been a wildlife research biologist with the Michigan Department of Natural Resources since 1964. He holds both a B.S. and M.S. degree in wildlife management from Michigan State University. Most of Ozoga's professional career has been spent at the Cusino Wildlife Research Station in Upper Michigan, where he and other research personnel of the Michigan DNR have conducted extensive studies on white-tailed deer.

Ozoga has authored or co-authored, at the time *Whitetail Country* was printed, 58 technical papers, which have appeared in such distinguished scientific publications as the *Journal of Wildlife Management*, the *Journal of Mammalogy*, and the *American Journal of Anatomy*. Although the majority of his published papers have concerned white-tailed deer ecology, physiology, nutrition, behavior and population dynamics, his scientific works also include papers on small mammals, foxes, coyotes, bears, and elk. In addition, he has had more than 20 popular articles published in various sporting and nature magazines in the last three years.

Ozoga resides in rural Munising, Michigan, with his wife, Janice. They have three sons and one daughter, all of whom, like their parents, share a strong attachment to the north country.

ACKNOWLEDGEMENTS

This book could not have been accomplished without the kind cooperation of many people. Above all, I'm deeply indebted to Dan Cox for the superb photography which so accurately depicts the behavior of white-tailed deer, the subject of this book.

My wife, Janice, faithfully assisted me with hundreds of hours of sometimes tedious and oftentimes uncomfortable observational studies. And if not for her foresight and encouragement, such popularization of white-tailed deer research findings on my behalf would never have come to be. Our youngsters, John, Holly, Mark, and Keith, all lent a helping hand when called upon, sometimes reluctantly so, but they cheerfully tolerated a household where the subject of white-tailed deer normally dominated conversation.

I'm particularly grateful to the many Michigan Department of Natural Resources personnel who assisted me through the years with data collection and analysis, handling deer during our annual Cusino enclosure trap-out census, reviewing manuscripts, and with other varied tasks. My sincere thanks, in particular, to present and past staff members of the Cusino Wildlife Research Station, including Louis Verme, biologist in charge, a research colleague of mine for nearly 25 years. Craig Benz, Rodney Clute, Dan DeLisle, and Leo Perry all served expertly in various capacities, frequently under hectic and trying circumstances. Carl Bennett Jr., Research Supervisor for the Wildlife Division, has done a yeoman's job maintaining a viable research program through some austere times.

For reading the manuscript and offering suggestions for its improvement, I wish to thank Carl Bennett Jr., Ed Langaneau Jr., Larry Marchinton, Janice Ozoga, and Louis Verme. I also wish to thank editor Chuck Petrie for this opportunity to express my views; he's been extremely helpful, patient, and a pleasure to work with.

The research work herein was funded in part by Michigan Federal Aid Wildlife Restoration Project W-127-R, and the Cusino Wildlife Research Station.

John J. Ozoga

PREFACE

No mammal in the world has likely attracted more attention, stirred more controversy, or has been so intensively investigated as the adaptable white-tailed deer (*Odocoileus virginianus*), a species that has not only survived in the wake of modern man's devastation, but has thrived and greatly expanded its traditional range in the Americas. Today, the elusive whitetail, represented by 38 subspecies, fares well from the arctic prairies in southern Canada, southward through the boreal and temperate forests, and into tropical forests of the Amazon River in Brazil.

Today, wildlife biologists know how to manipulate habitat and control deer population size to benefit whitetails, and they do so with reasonable success. Most managers are keenly aware, however, that "...techniques and methods constantly need refining and that solving of current problems often brings to light unforseen complexities" (Halls 1984:783). Among professional biologists, at any rate, there is a recognized need for more and better information concerning most facets of white-tailed deer life history, to assure this valuable resource is *wisely* managed.

Nutrition clearly controls the growth, reproduction, and survival of white-tailed deer throughout their extensive range, and the extreme importance of a proper balance between food and cover availability and numbers of deer has been repeatedly demonstrated and extensively investigated. However, the serious need for a more complete understanding of the species' social behavior was brought to my attention in the early 1970s when Anthony B. Bubenik, an internationally recognized authority on ungulate sociobiology, warned that behavioral and social factors might impact the welfare of certain hooved mammals just as effectively as do nutritional factors. Bubenik argued that free-choice hunting and the virtual elimination of major predators have seriously reduced the quality of ungulate populations around the globe. He also complained that most of today's harvest management systems regularly permit cropping of too many prime-age, healthy, highly fecund individuals — mortality that contrasts sharply with the predominantly selective culling by natural predators of young, old, and unhealthy individuals — and poor-quality animals thus survive longer and more of them breed, lowering the genetic vigor of the population.

Needless to say, these ideas were in direct conflict with traditional big game management philosophy and practice. In fact, many biologists in this country viewed such theory with skepticism and challenged Bubenik's contentions for their lack of supporting scientific evidence.

The basis for Bubenik's concerns rests on the premise that all mammals have evolved some form of social system to minimize tension and strife among individuals, a system that promotes an orderly way of life (or state of social "well-being") and assures genetic fitness within the population. Theoretically, overharvest of prime-age ungulates upsets the so-called "agonistic balance." Presumably, when mature animals are in short supply and are too few in number to dampen the aggressiveness of younger members, strife, excitement, and confusion can become dangerously intense and energetically costly to the society. Such disorder may then contribute to higher than normal food requirements, low productivity, and poor physical condition of the individuals in the population, and ultimately to severe damage to the animals' environment.

Logically, the white-tailed deer's societal organization originated as an adaptation to ecosystems in which the animals evolved, and, as such, is essential to the species' survival — an intriguing thought for the serious student of deer behavior to ponder. Conceivably, then, any phenomenon that tends to disrupt important behavioral patterns, such as unusual crowding or untimely mortality among certain sex-age classes, may ultimately be detrimental to the species' welfare, a possibility that we've been researching in the square-mile enclosure at the Cusino Wildlife Research Station, a Michigan Department of Natural Resources facility located near Shingleton, in Upper Michigan.

Only a decade ago, biologists knew surprisingly little about many aspects of the whitetail's social life, largely because earlier investigations had dealt almost exclusively with deer of unknown age or kinship, and most studies were complicated by uncontrollable changes in population density and structure due to nutritional factors, predation, or hunting-induced mortality. The Cusino enclosure has provided the opportunity to study the interrelationship of deer behavior and herd dynamics under "natural" yet highly controlled conditions, a unique compromise between studying deer closely confined in small pens and those that are completely free-ranging.

All deer within Cusino's fenced-in area are live-trapped and handled each March, an annual event that allows us to closely examine each animal, complete a population census, carefully control population size, and manipulate herd composition according to a predetermined study design. At trap-out, each animal is weighed, measured, blood-sampled to assess their physical condition and blood hormone level, ear-tagged and marked with a numbered ear pennant for individual field recognition. And depending upon specific study objectives, certain deer are fitted with radio transmitters for detailed behavior study. Surplus deer are released into the wild. We supplement the herd's natural diet with unlimited nutritious artificial feed year-round, to assure that nutrition *per se* is not a limiting factor in the herd's physical and reproductive performance.

By far, our most valuable data have been gathered by X-raying does in March. Fetuses, then 80 to 140 days old, are readily detectable on radiograms. In addition to providing an exact count of the number of fawns each doe carries, we've also devised methods to age the fetal images with surprising accuracy. Therefore, the x-ray technique has permitted us to calculate probable breeding and birth dates, accurately determine potential fawn production and, when coupled with field observations, assess fawn-rearing success of each individual doe under conditions of tightly controlled nutrition, known herd density, and closely regulated social-kinship arrangements, something not possible in other studies of free-ranging deer.

Through the years, we've gained considerable insight into the whitetail's life-style, documented the consequences of population-density-related social stress, and tested the effects of certain harvest management strategies. In a nutshell, we learned that the whitetail's social environment can indeed be a potent force influencing deer behavior and reproductive performance. In many respects, the consequences of social stress are quite similar to those of poor nutrition, as both factors can adversely impact deer health, reproduction, and survival, to the point of drastically slowing the population's rate of increase.

Fortunately, white-tailed deer exhibit immense behavioral plasticity, and in our studies were quite capable of coping with rather dramatic short-term changes in herd density and social structure caused by (simulated) hunting mortality. In fact, overpopulation stood out as the most serious threat to deer welfare, indicating that reasonable hunter harvesting of both sexes of deer is not only possible but absolutely necessary to maintain healthy and thriving deer populations.

I must emphasize, however, that we've barely scratched the surface in our studies of deer sociobiology and that many important questions remain unanswered. The long-term, potentially deleterious effects of prolonged social disruption caused by hunter selectivity of the "best" specimens, in particular, are unknown, making further in-depth study necessary before certain intensive harvest management strategies can be continued — or others implemented — with confidence.

Nonetheless, despite the tone of these introductory pages, this book is not about deer hunting — I make no mention of rifle ballistics, camouflage clothing, hunting tactics, or the like. *Whitetail Country* concerns, as I perceive them after more than 25 years of study, seasonal variations in white-tailed deer behavior that are vital to the species healthful existence. My treatise here should be of interest to anyone interested in the behavior and welfare of this magnificent and amazing creature. However, I sincerely hope that hunters, in particular, find new insights in these pages, and as a result, become more appreciative of the vital role that they play in determining this species' quality of life.

The excellent photography by Daniel Cox in this volume clearly depicts the behavioral strengths and weaknesses of whitetails in the northern environment. And, although the whitetail is sometimes portrayed as a vicious, agonistic beast — as the mature animal can be — keep in mind that white-tailed deer have evolved behavioral traits that permit them to live peaceably with members of their own kind and in reasonable harmony with the environment, oftentimes under seemingly stressful and hostile circumstances.

The text for *Whitetail Country* is based primarily upon findings of research conducted at Michigan's Cusino Wildlife Research Station, but I've also made liberal use of other pertinent literature, much of which is listed in the selected reference section of this book for the benefit of those interested in further reading. Herein lies my current thinking, knowing full well that my ideas and integration of certain information may not be viewed favorably by some experts in the field of deer research or management. In that regard, I anxiously await new research findings or better interpretations by those more knowledgeable about white-tailed deer behavior than I.

John J. Ozoga
13 January 1988

CONTENTS

The snows have receded, revealing both victims and gaunt survivors of the harsh northern winter, the season that culls the sick, the lame, and other unfit animals from whitetail herds. For the survivors, however, a season of plenty is close at hand.

SPRING

For white-tailed deer, throughout their extensive range in North America, spring is typically a season of increasing warmth and abundant nutritious foods. By early May, even the dense old-growth northern hardwood forests — at other seasons nearly devoid of good deer foods — are carpeted with a thick mat of adder's-tongue, spring beauties, dutchman's breeches, violets, trilliums, and assorted showy spring flora. Indeed, for deer, spring is a season of plenty, in the form of lush herbaceous growth that is readily digestible for energy needs and is rich in protein, essential minerals, and vitamins. And fortunately so because spring is a season of great nutritional requirements for all deer, young and old, and especially for the unborn.

With the lengthening of daylight hours (photoperiod), deer become more active. Their metabolism shifts, from its low, almost semi-hibernation, level during mid-winter, back to a comparatively high summertime rate. Thereafter, steadily increasing energy demands associated with resumption of body growth in young deer, new antler growth among adult bucks, and the advanced development of fetuses carried by pregnant does rapidly sap any scant internal energy stores that deer might still possess following the critical winter season of food scarcity.

Early spring — that narrow interval between winter and the fawning season — represents a highly sociable time of year for whitetails. On northern range, in particular, large mixed associations comprised of both sexes and all age-classes of deer can be seen foraging peaceably together on fresh new grasses and forbs as deer first break free from the confines of their winter "yards." To the uninformed, such complex aggregations would hint that the species lacked any semblance of social order.

To the contrary, however, white-tailed deer have evolved some rather fascinating behavior patterns in order to cope with environmental stresses and have their own strict form of social organization that provides for an orderly and efficient way of life. It's a system that permits rapid exploitation of available food and cover resources and allows them to live in harmony with one another and their environment.

Among adults, bucks and does live apart — socially speaking at any rate — except during the rut, and of course in winter wherever cold weather and deep snow force them to seek out and congregate in the best sheltered sites available.

Mature bucks (those two years and older) join fraternal groups composed of two to six, and sometimes more, compatible males. Usually these bucks are unrelated, but they soon learn to recognize one another by sight and smell, and develop true social bonds. Normally found together during spring, summer, and winter, bucks tend to be solitary travelers during the autumn breeding season.

The basic social organization in female whitetails, on the other hand, consists of a family group composed of a matriarch doe, several generations of her daughters and their fawns. Several such related female groups share a common ancestral range and, at times, band together as a close-knit clan. Peak levels of re-grouping occur during harsh weather in winter, when the females and young of an entire clan may unite in protective cover. In effect, the female whitetail likely spends her entire lifetime in close association with female relatives.

In the South, or wherever winters are not severe, the spring shuffle calls for only minor adjustments in the whitetail's daily routine. Southern deer may temporarily shift their center of activity to take advantage of seasonal changes in food availability or to find temporary relief from inclement weather, but they seldom leave the boundaries of their home range for lengthy periods. Food scarcity tends to increase the size of their home range, but most live within an area 100 to 800 acres in size.

It's a different story at the northern extremity of the whitetail's geographic range, where deer occupy wintertime ranges that are oftentimes widely separated from those held in summer. In northern Michigan, for example, deer travel, on average, eight to nine miles (sometimes up to 40 miles) between preferred wintering habitat and their traditional summering grounds.

Spring migration usually takes place in March or April, just as soon as temperatures moderate and snow depths recede sufficiently to permit easy travel. However, the onset and duration of such movement will vary greatly from one year to the next and between areas, depending on climatic factors. Deer may spend days or even weeks in migration.

In early spring, even sap flowing from trees may be a form of sustenance for whitetails.
This buck, still shedding his winter coat, licks the sweet, running fluid from the bark of a maple.

More prolonged migratory trips tend to occur when deer leave the wintering area early in spring and when long travel distances are involved.

Where deer seasonally migrate considerable distances, young animals rely upon older female relatives for guidance. Apparently, fawns must be led from summer to winter range in early winter, and back again in spring, before they fully learn lengthy migration routes. Without adult leadership, some young deer have been know to wander aimlessly in spring before finally settling in strange habitat.

Adult deer are extremely traditional in their habits and have strong attachment to their summertime home ranges, returning to the same areas year after year. In fact, where a deer lives is generally determined more by its early social experience, learning, and traditional habits than due to some mystical inherent ability to select the best habitat available to them.

Adult bucks and does are separated not only socially but also spatially during much of the year. There is good evidence that the bucks tend to occupy the poorer quality habitat in summer, whereas females more likely rear their fawns in areas with the greatest abundance of nutritious foods. But during that brief period in spring before fawns are born, the two societies (buck and doe) travel, with minimum conflict, sizeable overlapping ranges while in search of choice foods.

Bucks that are in good health show new antler growth beginning in April. And because antlers may elongate at the astounding rate of more than one-half inch per day (making them one of the fastest-growing structures in the animal kingdom), given good nutrition, some bucks may display full-sized velvet antlers by late July. Those individuals in poor health, however, usually show delayed antler development.

Although velvet antlers are extremely delicate and easily damaged, bucks seem to possess certain special senses that permit them to judge their own rack size and shape. Furthermore, the live antler is richly supplied with sensory nerves, and the velvet hairs seem to serve as touch-sensitive feelers that warn in advance of a pending collision. Even large-antlered bucks can move rapidly and gracefully through dense forest cover, and surprisingly few of them show signs of velvet antler damage. Fortunately, antler growth takes place when production of the male hormone testosterone, an androgen which triggers aggression, is at a low level. This likely accounts for the bucks' easy-going nature and tendency to avoid conflict during spring and summer, which also minimizes the chances of damaging growing antlers.

On northern range, most whitetail fawns are born in late May or early June (following a 200-day gestation period), whereas peak fawning in southern states is a week to several weeks later, where it's also more protracted. In certain sections of the country, such as the fertile farmlands of the Midwest — where climate is favorable, deer density is relatively low, and deer enjoy abundant nutritious foods year-round — roughly half of the females

Spring's warmer temperatures, rains, and lengthening daylight periods herald the growth of new, lush green vegetation in the forest meadows. The new growth, in turn, provides whitetails the food source they will rely upon for the coming year.

can be expected to achieve an advanced rate of physical maturation and produce their first fawn(s) when about one year old. These young mothers generally fawn about a month later than older does.

The maternally experienced doe gradually restricts her foraging activity to that of her traditional fawning grounds. She'll usually show some signs of udder enlargement anywhere from two weeks to several days before fawning. And a few days before giving birth, she isolates herself by driving away all other deer, including her year-old fawns. Should her newborn fawns survive, the mother becomes amazingly secretive, boldly aggressive towards neighboring deer (even mature bucks), and adopts a form of territorial behavior that will last four to six weeks.

Initially, territory boundary disputes probably involve some rather violent, aggressive interactions. However, the whitetail's usual repertoire of defensive and threat behaviors is stereotyped and non-contact in nature, including the "ear-drop, hard-look" display, which consists of a cold stare, with ears laid back and head held high or low. Lack of a submissive response to this threat display commonly leads to "kicking" or "slapping" with the foreleg and is sometimes followed by "chasing." When two does (or antlerless bucks) of comparable dominance rank encounter, they may "flail," wherein the contestants rear up on their hind legs and kick at one another with their front feet.

Once dominance is achieved, some form of scent marking (possibly via urine and feces) by the dominant doe then likely serves to delineate her territory, although this aspect of deer behavior is poorly understood. Whatever the mechanisms involved, subordinates seem to get the message and learn to recognize and willingly avoid these grounds.

Young does fawning for their first time behave in a similar manner. Each one sets-up and defends a fawning (parturition) territory, border to border with that of their mother. And as the family group increases in number, crowding over a period of years causes second-time mothers (usually those three years old) to disperse a short distance — of a quarter-mile or so — to establish new fawning grounds. This intricate system of territory formation helps the matriarch preserve her traditional fawning area, benefits the young inexperienced doe and her offspring in various ways, and also provides for an orderly expansion of a clan's range during "good times."

However, radio-tracking studies of transmitter-equipped does have revealed that the dispersing doe incurs considerable risk and competition for space when dispersing to new grounds. Dispersers oftentimes settle in unsuitable fawning habitat or attempt to rear fawns within another doe's territory. These dispersing does commonly experience higher newborn fawn losses than non-dispersing individuals.

During the period when nursing does staunchly defend their fawning territories, which are generally about 10 to 20 acres in size, non-reproducing yearlings (male and female) occupy the travel-free corridors that normally exist between adjacent territories. Nonetheless, if a doe's newborn fawns should die, the mother resumes a sociable lifestyle within a few days. In that event she becomes more active, travels a larger range, likely centers her activities in a different part of her home range, and allows her yearling as well as other non-productive female relatives (daughters that have also lost their fawns) to

*For whitetails and most other forest dwellers, spring is the season of birth. Here,
lying on the forest floor, her facial expression indicating her condition,
a whitetail doe winces in pain during the early stages of labor.*

accompany her.

Deer living in the savannah grasslands of Texas reportedly behave differently than those living in forested habitat. In the open grasslands, does usually leave their newborn fawns in hiding while they themselves graze with other deer. The differing maternal-care strategies, which apparently evolved in response to sharply contrasting environmental circumstances, allow whitetails in forested and non-forested habitats to cope most effectively with the constant threat that predation poses to the survival of their vulnerable offspring.

Parturition territorial behavior restricts the number of successful does in a given area of forested habitat, as no two can simultaneously occupy the same acreage to raise young. Thus, such behavior promotes population self-regulation, constituting a density-dependent mechanism that limits population size even when nutrition is not limited. Because dominance among female whitetails is closely age-related, wherein older does attain the highest rank, older mothers usually secure the best fawning habitat available and are invariably more successful in raising fawns when space is limited. In fact, if herd density is sufficiently high (over 100 deer per square mile) many first-time mothers may abandon otherwise healthy offspring purely because of crowding, lack of parturition solitude, and resultant psychological stress.

The doe gives birth, either while standing or in a prostrate position, with seemingly little regard to the exact location or specific vegetative characteristics within her normal fawning range. Fawns are sometimes born in grassy openings, but on other occasions are "dropped" in heavily wooded or brushy cover. Usually, however, dry upland sites seem to be preferred over low wetlands.

A whitetail buck exhibits a threat display to a younger male to drive it from a feeding area. When the ears-laid-back signal fails to convey its message, the larger deer drives its forelegs down on the intruding buck's back and continues the attack, biting the smaller deer's ear.

Siblings are generally born about 15 to 20 minutes apart, and twins are the rule, but triplets are common, and even quintuplets have been reported. However, first-time mothers and older does that were poorly nourished the previous autumn are more likely to have a single fawn. And, contrary to the "old dry-doe" myth, even does 12 years of age and older regularly produce viable offspring.

The mother spends four to six hours following parturition at the birth site with her newborn. She cleans them of amniotic fluids and membranes and carefully consumes all traces of the afterbirth (a trait not exhibited by all members of the deer family). Even the vegetation stained during the birth process is eaten, oftentimes rendering the picked-over birth site quite recognizable as such — at least to the trained eye. This careful cleansing serves to minimize odors that might otherwise attract predators, and scientists speculate that the ingested amniotic membranes might supply the doe with certain important nutrients.

The fawn nurses almost immediately, generally while the mother lies on her side. Colostrum milk, the high-protein secretion produced by the doe for a short time after giving birth, also provides the antibodies necessary to resist disease until the fawn's own immune system begins to function.

Isolation of the mother and newborn and the doe's grooming of the fawn shortly after birth are essential in establishing the mother-infant bond (imprinting). Any disturbance during this critical period can lead to a breakdown in the imprinting process and can contribute to abandonment and death of the young. The risk is greatest when maternally inexperienced (young) does are involved. The mother seems to imprint upon her young within a few hours, but it may be several days before the newborn fawns become fully imprinted upon their mother. During the interim, the impressionable newborn risk being attracted to almost any large moving object — even humans — which necessitates their early solitary existence.

Animals characteristically produce more young than can be expected to survive. White-tailed deer are no exception. For one reason or another, a large portion of the fawns born annually fail to survive their first few weeks. By far the most important factor

influencing a newborn whitetail's prospects for survival is its birth weight, which in turn hinges upon the mother's nutritional status during pregnancy. Careful investigations of pen-confined does, conducted by Lou Verme at the Cusino Wildlife Research Station in Upper Michigan, revealed that over 90 percent of the offspring born to does malnourished throughout pregnancy died shortly after birth. In contrast, roughly 95 percent of those born to well-fed mothers survived. Survivors, on average, weighed about eight pounds, whereas those that died weighed about four pounds at birth.

The controlled studies revealed that malnourished does rarely absorbed or aborted fetuses, but that stillbirths of full-term young were quite common. The bulk of fawn mortality consisted of animals born alive but stunted in size and either too weak to stand or too small to nurse, or of fawns born to mothers that had no milk. Most such runts perished within a day or two.

Other researchers found that compared to well-fed does, poorly nourished ones also more readily abandoned their offspring. Many of these malnourished mothers wouldn't groom their newborn, failed to eat the afterbirth, or refused to nurse. Some does even showed fear of their own fawns. Another investigator learned that predators usually killed more newborn fawns following severe winters, largely because does in poor health were less inclined to defend their young. In either case — abandonment or lack of maternal defense — such abnormal behavior likely arises because of a hormonal imbalance (possibly insufficient production of prolactin, a protein hormone that induces milk secretion) that is brought on by malnutrition and which tends to disrupt basic maternal instincts.

Healthy whitetail fawns weigh six to nine pounds at birth (southern subspecies weigh somewhat less) and are generally walking within 20 to 30 minutes. Despite their wobbly appearance, healthy fawns are capable of traveling several hundred yards, with motherly encouragement, within a few hours. Although siblings are born at the same site, the mother leads them to widely spaced (100 to 400 feet apart) bed sites within her pre-selected territory soon after the initial bout of nursing and grooming. Those fawns that are malformed or too small and weak to leave the birth site, though, may risk immediate abandonment.

Although infant whitetails are typically obedient creatures highly dependent upon their mother's guidance, some succumb to fences, mud holes, drowning, and a host of other accidents that might befall inquisitive and ungainly forest babies. On average, about 10 percent of any given whitetail fawn crop can be expected to die as the result of stillbirths, birth defects, and accidents shortly after birth, even when the mothers are well nourished and predators are scarce.

Disease and parasitism seldom pose a serious threat to newborn fawn survival on northern range. In the South, it's frequently a different story. In Texas, for example, bacterial infections of the genus *Salmonella* (referred to as salmonellosis) have peri-

This doe, a victim of a freak accident, lies dead at the bottom of a forest ravine.
Having lain down at the edge of the slope above the small valley to give birth to her fawn, the doe's
thrashing during her labor caused her to topple off the edge and into the ravine. At the bottom,
her slide was halted by a dead tree, breaking her neck.

Whitetails give birth either lying down or, less typically, standing. This doe is undergoing a normal delivery, her fawn emerging muzzle and front feet first from her womb. As the amniotic sack breaks, its fluids spill out and the fawn can be seen gasping its first breath. Further contractions of the womb force the fawn's shoulders out and, eventually, the rest of its tiny body. The umbilical cord remains attached for a short period while the mother rests from her labor. Later, the doe will eat the umbilical cord and the afterbirth, removing any trace of this event that could lead predators to her young.

Following pages: A whitetail doe rests with one of her newborn fawns as the other makes one of its first attempts to stand and walk.

odically caused high death rates among newborn whitetails. The causative organism, acquired by ingestion, spreads through the bloodstream. The bacteria are transmitted through the feces to other hosts.

Salmonellosis occurs almost exclusively in fawns and may assume two basic forms. In one form, death may occur before diarrhea develops. A fawn thus sick will fail to groom itself, leading to ruffled hair and a generally unkempt appearance. Dehydration causes the skin about the face to tighten, the eyes appear sunken, and the animal weakens rapidly. Soon it is unable to stand, and death occurs within a few hours. The other form of salmonellosis appears in more-disease-resistant fawns — generally those a few weeks old — which develop diarrhea within 12 to 24 hours following infection. In the wild, these infected fawns are oftentimes found simply lying in the grass, showing evidence of diarrhea.

Likewise, heavy infestations of the lone-star tick (*Amblyomma americanum*) can cause anemia and high death rates among young whitetails. Tick bites around the eyes and

head, in particular, lead to blindness and ultimately to the death of the parasitized fawn. In 1968, investigators found some deer literally covered with the larvae, nymphs, and adult stages of the tick at the Cookson Hill Wildlife Refuge in eastern Oklahoma, and estimated that 34 percent of the newborn fawns in that area died from this infestation.

Whitetails, both fawns and adults, are also vulnerable to a variety of infectious diseases. Among the viral diseases is epizootic hemorrhagic disease (EHD). This disease, for which there is no known effective treatment or means of control, is believed to be transmitted by blood-sucking gnats. Often referred to as "bluetongue," EHD is potentially devastating. Although outbreaks of EHD may periodically appear in the North, the disease erupts almost annually in the Southwest, where it sometimes kills large numbers of deer within relatively small geographic areas. Deer are also inflicted with certain bacterial diseases such as anthrax, enterotoxemia, brucellosis, and leptospirosis, as well as certain fungal infections such as actinomycosis, or "lumpy jaw." Such maladies, EHD included, are most prevalent in southern states during late summer or early autumn and are frequently associated with high deer densities.

Predation is another factor that depletes the numbers of young whitetails. Many meat-eaters, such as wolves, coyotes, bobcats, bears, mountain lions, and even domestic dogs, prey upon fawns. However, the whitetail doe's territorial behavior — wide spacing of siblings, mother-infant separation, and relatively long-distance movements between consecutive bed sites during the young fawn's "hider" phase — incorporates sound anti-predator strategies common to certain other members of the deer family.

The young fawn's own chief defense against predation is "hiding," and its speckled coat blends in perfectly with flecks of sunlight that filter through overhead vegetative

*Twin fawns nurse from their mother. Early in spring, if a doe has twin fawns,
she will only nurse one fawn at a time, two or three times a day. When the fawns are older,
as these are, they often nurse simultaneously. By the time the young deer are 10 to 12 weeks old,
however, they will be weaned and dependent upon vegetation for sustenance.*

cover, providing ideal camouflage. When in danger the fawn instinctively "freezes," exhibiting a depressed physiological state referred to as alarm bradycardia, wherein its breathing and heart rate decrease sharply — an adaptation that further minimizes the chances of attracting predator attention.

The mother visits, grooms, and nurses her young fawns (separately) only two or three times daily. The fawn nurses (about eight ounces per meal) excitedly, its tail waggling, while standing in transverse, head to tail, position with the mother. The mother's simultaneous grooming of the youngster's anal area stimulates the fawn to defecate and urinate at the nursing site. Following each care session the fawn is led 200 to 400 feet to a fresh, odorless bed site.

Although the young fawn spends much of its time in hiding, "lying low" for as much as 12 hours at a time, when given the proper signals, which may include the mother's soft plaintive mewing and gentle nudging, even the unsteady fawn only a few hours old becomes an obedient and diligent "follower." As a result, within relatively few days, the young fawn is introduced to its mother's fawning range. Thereafter, whenever disturbed or threatened by predators, the fawn flees, but not haphazardly; it stays within its familiar area, where maternal rescue is more likely.

The mother normally maintains an alert vigil while concealed in thick cover — a necessary component of favorable whitetail fawning habitat — usually within a few hundred feet of her resting fawn. If threatened, the distressed fawn's bawl brings mother running to the rescue within seconds. It's interesting to note, however, that the doe can not readily distinguish the calls of her own fawns from those of strange individuals. Neither can she easily recognize them visually. Early in life, odor seems to be the only sure means of identification. Therefore, especially when doe fawning territories are closely aligned, it's not unusual to see two, or sometimes even three, does rush to defend a bawling fawn. Such behavior likely proves especially beneficial to the young inexperienced mother and her offspring, as the matriarch may on occasion lend some timely, albeit unintentional, defense against predators.

Oftentimes even a strange fawn's distant distress call will cause a tentative doe to quickly check the well-being of her own offspring. And if need be, she'll relocate the young by leading them to the safety of dense cover.

Because major deer predators such as coyotes hunt primarily by sight, some investigators theorize that the lack of good ground level hiding cover for fawns leads to excessive losses from predation in some areas. In fact, high newborn fawn death rates (in excess of 80 percent) that sometimes occur in sparsely vegetated sectors of the Southwest are commonly attributed to heavy predation by coyotes. By comparison, in the farmlands of the Midwest, where pregnant does are well nourished and vegetation at fawn bedding sites tends to be much thicker, newborn fawn losses seldom exceed 30 percent.

Early in a fawn's existence, before it is strong and agile enough to escape danger, it spends much of its life, sometimes up to 12 hours a day, in hiding. During this period, the motionless fawn's camouflage coat and its mother's defense are all that protect it from predators.

Disease, predation, accidents, and, sometimes, abandonment by their mothers make fawns' survival tenuous at best. A majority of the deer born in a given spring usually survive, but events and circumstances during the first two months of a fawn's life are critical to its continued existence.

Nonetheless, other studies have demonstrated that maternally experienced does may purposely position their fawns in openings where a predator's presence might more easily be detected and the mother can rush swiftly to the fawn's aid when necessary. All things considered, an interspersed cover arrangement with some openings as well as dense cover probably makes the most ideal fawn-rearing habitat for whitetails.

Does normally keep their fawns within the boundaries of a prescribed territory during the first month. However, given a serious "near miss" predator encounter, the concerned prime-age mother may lead her young to a temporary new location as much as a half-mile outside of her usual fawning grounds. Such behavior seems to occur less frequently among young does, possibly because their comparatively low dominance status prevents them from trespassing upon the territories of older, more-dominant females. The displaced mother and her fawns usually return to their normal range within a few days, presumably once the serious threat of predation passes.

Among the maternal-care strategies employed by white-tailed deer, outright defense of their offspring against predators may be as important as any single factor influencing fawn survival. Irate does have been known to charge and strike at coyotes and domestic dogs, and even humans, in defense of their fawns. And the more-experienced mother may sometimes display complex distraction behavior, similar to the broken-wing act of a brooding grouse, in an attempt to entice predators away from fawns. I've never personally been struck by a doe, but admittedly have, on numerous occasions, been distracted by them as they've crashed recklessly around me in ever-tightening circles while I handled a bawling fawn.

Quite clearly, the newborn whitetail's prospects for survival are controlled by the mother: Bed site habitat, movement patterns, social and spacial relationships, and

evasive tactics when threatened by predators are all aspects of the doe's maternal behavior. Studies conducted in the Cusino enclosure revealed that prime-aged does (those four years and older), because of their high dominance status, more easily held previously established, favorable fawning habitat. And compared to younger does, they spaced littermates farther apart (thus minimizing the chances of a predator killing the entire litter), moved fawns greater distances from one bed site to the next, and despite maintaining a more distant vigil, responded swiftly to defend their young.

Prime-aged does even responded defensively to artificially induced predator odor. When we placed coyote urine in the vicinity of their bedded, radio-transmitter-equipped fawns, radio telemetry studies showed older mothers moved their young about twice as far as they would in a normal move from one bed site to the next. But such treatment had no obvious effect upon the behavior of younger does and their fawns.

Although newborn fawn death rates increased sharply within the Cusino enclosure when black bears unexpectedly entered the compound — rising from 10 percent to 32 percent annually — young does (two and three years old) suffered three to four times greater fawn losses than did prime-aged mothers. Experienced mothers rarely lost single fawns or both members of twin litters, whereas complete litter failure among young does was not uncommon.

We could never prove it, but circumstantial evidence strongly implied that maternally experienced does more readily challenged predators — even bears — when their young were threatened, and were apparently quite successful in doing so. At any rate, regardless of the variables involved, we found older does to be far better mothers, indicating that learning experience plays an important part in better mothering "instincts."

Given the mother's good health, and favorable nutrition, whitetail fawns grow rapidly — doubling their weight within two weeks. (Compared with cow's milk, deer milk is richer in fat, protein, dry solids, and energy.) During this two-week period, the fawns' prospects for survival virtually increase day by day, and their behavior changes accordingly.

By late spring, deer become settled in their favored traditional summer habitat. Although the yearlings, adult bucks, and non-productive does continue to socialize in small groups, nursing does and fawns, which represent a large segment of any healthy deer herd, remain solitary, secretive, and inconspicuous. The fawns will grow and learn during summer, progressing through various transitional stages of activity and behavior, developing from relatively helpless suckling infants nutritionally dependent on their mothers to fairly independent, metabolically weaned ruminants by late summer. But during late spring and early summer the screening effects of dense vegetation, coupled with the whitetail's shy and sedentary nature, may make deer seem practically nonexistent where they live at low densities.

Early in a fawn's life its mother can not audibly or visually distinguish it from the fawns of other does. Odor seems to be the only way a doe can identify her own fawns. Here, a hungry fawn errantly approaches a doe it has mistaken for its mother, to nurse. The doe, by smelling the fawn, determines that it is not her offspring, and, when the fawn reaches for her teats, rejects it with a gentle kick.

For most forest animals, including whitetail deer, summer is a time when food availability is at its peak. During this relatively peaceful period, deer spend a majority of their time resting, feeding and ruminating, building up energy reserves for the autumn breeding season and the following winter.

SUMMER

Summer in whitetail country is a tranquil, almost lazy time. It is a season of spotted fawns, sleek red-coated does, and lethargic, well-mannered bucks with bulging, velvet antlers. Deer are rather evenly distributed across their range in summer, and all seem to share the same obsession — eating. The late summer and early autumn months are when young deer strive for maximum growth. It is during this period, too, that adults replenish spent energy stores in preparation for another enervating breeding season and the stressful winter period to follow.

The white-tailed deer's summertime diet will vary greatly, from one area to the next, depending primarily on what foods are available. They've been known to eat just about anything at one time or another, ranging from mushrooms and lichens to fish and insects, but have the remarkable ability to select the best, most nutritious foods available, switching to less-palatable and less-nourishing items as the preferred ones decline. Green leafy browse becomes more important in the deer's summer diet as forb abundance decreases and grasses mature and dry. And of course, whenever available, whitetails eagerly supplement their natural diet with nutritious farm crops.

Early summer food resources are normally adequate for deer throughout most of their range, but there are exceptions. Some habitat types are far better than others, while certain areas are consistently poor because of infertile soils. The best deer range will have

Bucks and does occupy different areas during the summer. Buck groups traditionally reside in areas of marginal habitat, but fawn-rearing does and their young, which require greater amounts of protein and other vital nutrients as a result of lactation and rapid growth, respectively, inhabit areas where higher-quality foods are available.

great diversity in habitat characteristics and contain a wide variety of grasses, weeds, shrubs and trees. This allows deer to select a variety of foods and change their feeding habits in response to changes in forage availability, without greatly increasing their radius of travel.

Deer overabundance can also adversely impact habitat quality. Because whitetails are selective feeders, an expanding deer herd can drastically reduce or even eliminate certain choice natural herbage that is readily digestible and rich in protein. At the same time, other plants may increase either because they're less palatable, resistant to grazing, or both. Consequently, range severely overgrazed by white-tailed deer may not exhibit the stark overused appearance one would expect. Even so, the land's nutritional base and capacity to naturally support healthy deer steadily declines with continued overuse.

The nursing whitetail doe, in particular, is under considerable nutritional stress while at peak lactation in early summer. Even those does that are well-nourished might devote as much as 70 percent of their time to foraging, and favorable food conditions are critically important in order for them to achieve maximum milk production as well as to maintain their own physical vigor. If nutrition is inadequate, the doe's milk yield tends to decline, even though the milk's quality in terms of chemical composition remains fairly constant. Reduced milk yield, however, results in poor growth among young fawns, and on occasion their starvation has been reported from arid regions of deer overabundance where summer drought limits forage availability.

When only a few days old, fawns begin to nibble at vegetation, although they do not start to ruminate until they are about two weeks old. By five weeks of age fawns are dependent upon rumination, but they still rely on their mother's milk for sustenance. Although some fawns may nurse well into autumn, they're functionally weaned when 10 to 12 weeks old.

White-tailed deer usually have an elongate home range, which maximizes available food resources while minimizing travel and energy expenditure. The size of the home range will vary according to various environmental and behavioral factors, and considerable seasonal variation in size and configuration of the range can also be expected.

The amount of acreage occupied by individual deer during summer will be considerably smaller than is normally the case during other seasons. Except for yearling males, which sometimes wander quite extensively, most deer living in favorable habitat can probably satisfy their early summer needs within an area less than 200 acres in size. Nursing does, however, may restrict their activities to an area less than 40 acres in size until their fawns are six to eight weeks old.

Sharply reduced daily movement is characteristic of malnourished, sickly, or injured deer. However, even healthy animals spend considerable time bedded, most of which is spent ruminating or grooming. Some deer show strong preference for and repeated use of specific bedding locations. Others more likely use different bed sites each time. In summer, adult deer seldom remain bedded for more than two hours at a time, and interludes of sleep rarely last more than a few minutes.

Deer relish fresh water during hot weather but can survive on dew, temporary water from rain puddles, or by eating succulent vegetation. Most deer in the eastern United States have ready access to surface water of some type, but those living in arid regions of the Southwest may concentrate closer to permanent water areas during periods of extended drought.

Adult deer are strong swimmers and will easily cross sizeable streams and lakes. At times they may purposely seek out and consume certain emergent aquatic plants, or even partially submerge themselves to escape annoying insects. Drowning among young fawns, however, may be a significant mortality factor in some environments or during times of severe flooding.

During summer, adult bucks tend to live in separate groups and in separate areas from does. The males return to favored summer haunts year after year. In forested habitat, groups of two or three adult bucks generally share a common range, and larger groups of six to eight bucks are sometimes reported. (Bucks living in more open habitat commonly occur in large groups, the memberships of which are constantly changing.) Group members develop close bonds and seem to maintain a strict dominance hierarchy, even during summer, via bluffing and stereotyped non-contact threats. However, details of the whitetail buck's summer social life have not been intensively investigated, and are at best only poorly understood.

An otherwise tranquil period for white-tailed deer, summer's warm weather brings a variety of bothersome biting insects to whitetail country. Here, a young buck is harassed by a deerfly.

Mutual grooming appears to play an important role in whitetail social structure, especially in doe groups and between fawns and their mothers. These two red-coated does, members of the same matriarchal doe group, groom each other in what appears to be a tender yet ritualized procedure.

Depending primarily on deer herd composition and density, some yearlings that are driven away by their mothers may associate temporarily, and rather cautiously, with buck groups in summer. More often, however, they'll be found exclusively in yearling groups that concentrate their activities within familiar ancestoral range and travelling the vacant corridors that exist between adjacent doe's fawn-rearing territories. And as mentioned earlier, whenever newborn fawn losses are excessive, many yearlings will reunite almost immediately with their fawnless mothers, older sisters, or a combination of both, and accompany them throughout the summer. Yearling littermates usually remain together in summer, but the males may periodically take off on brief exploratory jaunts several miles into strange country.

As with certain other ungulates, whitetail bucks tend to occupy the marginal habitat in summer, whereas fawn-rearing does, and usually their yearlings, select the better habitat and a higher-quality diet. Within the Cusino enclosure, bucks favor the hilly, mature northern hardwoods that cover the area's northern perimeter. This is an area where sugar maple predominates in the tightly closed canopy and forms a thick mat of seedlings on the shaded forest floor. In contrast, enclosure does seem to avoid that sector, preferring instead to raise fawns in brushy areas more interspersed with openings that provide a greater mixture of forage species. But such sex differences in summer range occupation by whitetails are oftentimes subtle and may be unnoticeable in areas of great habitat diversity or wherever antlered bucks are so heavily harvested by hunters that few attain prime age.

Adult bucks normally weigh about 30 percent more than females and have a lower whole-body metabolic requirement per unit gut capacity. This difference presumably allows males to subsist on lower quality foods when nutritious ones become scarce. Females, however, seem unable to meet their energetic needs by filling up on less-nutritious foods even when they're profusely abundant.

During the period when bucks are living in isolated groups, their antlers grow rapidly. Mature healthy individuals may carry prominent antlers by early June and almost full-sized velvet racks by mid-July. Those in poor health, and yearlings, generally demonstrate somewhat delayed antler growth.

Antlers are status symbols of male supremacy — adornments that evolved hand in hand with certain aspects of deer breeding behavior. Large antlers are showy structures that permit bucks to display and advertise themselves, to attract prospective mates, and to intimidate rival males. Antlers serve an important role in highly ritualized sparring matches and the more-serious fighting among bucks sometimes necessary to decide dominance order and pre-determine mating privileges prior to the breeding season.

Although similarities between the two sides of a buck's rack — or even between one animal's rack and that of another — are often striking, no two antlers are exactly alike. An individual buck commonly has one antler with more tines than that of his opposite antler, and each antler's tines, which can grow at various angles, may be of different lengths than the corresponding tines on the opposite antler. Such differences make antlered bucks distinctive and permit deer to readily distinguish one buck from another, based on antler features alone.

The size of a buck's rack will vary depending upon the animal's age, his nutritional history, and inherited traits. Buck antler size and body size generally go together. That is, a big buck normally carries a large rack, whereas a small-bodied buck will more likely grow small antlers. Both antler and body size tend to increase with a buck's age and peak when he's between four and a half and eight and a half years old. Because body growth takes precedence over antler growth, however, any deficiency in dietary energy, protein, calcium, phosphorus, or certain vitamins during spring and summer can have profound negative effects upon antler length, mass, and number of points, particularly among young, growing bucks. Nutritional shortage in winter has less overall impact upon antler growth.

Many antler features such as rack shape, tine length and configuration, as well as other specific features, are unquestionably hereditary. Numerous examples exist where captive bucks have produced, year after year, antler sets that are very similar in appearance. Given good health, a mature buck's rack will grow a little larger and may add an extra point here and there with advancing age. Otherwise, subsequent antler sets will closely resemble one another.

Antler peculiarities, though, are strictly the result of chance. Skeletal injury, or direct injury to the tender, growing antler itself, can also produce abnormal antler formation, which shouldn't be confused with malformations caused by poor nutrition, extreme old age, or genetics. Genetically or nutritionally controlled antler abnormalities will usually

In summer, bucks' antlers, encased in their nutrient-supplying blood-engorged velvet,
are the fastest growing things known in the animal kingdom,
sometimes increasing in length by a half inch in a single day.

show on both sides of a buck's rack, but a one-sided oddity is more likely due to some type of injury.

One perplexing observation is what scientists refer to as "contralateral effects," where injuries to one side of a buck's body result in antler deformities on the opposite side. For example, if a buck happens to break its right hind leg, it will likely grow a short left antler, a response that may reappear for several years after the injury. Investigators consider many such reports valid and have demonstrated them experimentally, but they lack a sound biological explanation for these occurrences.

Psychological stress due to overpopulation, and subsequently the frequent conflicts that arise among deer, can also suppress antler growth among young bucks, even when nourishing foods are plentiful. Although the physiological mechanisms involved in this intriguing phenomenon are poorly understood, it appears that behavioral stress may lead to a deficiency in testosterone production or cause some type of hormonal disturbance that blocks its stimulating effects. Testosterone is critically important throughout the antler cycle and is absolutely essential for proper development of the buck's first antlers.

Before any deer can grow antlers, it must first grow pedicles — the "stumps" on which antlers form — which requires a certain threshold level of testosterone. Pedicles first show as a pair of cowlicks in the forehead pelage of very young male fawns. They can be felt as small, bony lumps beneath the skin and usually don't become pronounced "nubbins" until the fawn is four to five months old, at which time increased output of testosterone stimulates the laying down of additional bone at the pedicle sites.

Only the pedicle is capable of giving rise to a normal and complete antler. Injury to the pedicle may cause abnormal antler formation, or it may even lead to accessory antlers produced by the injured pedicle or nearby regions of the skull.

In the absence of testosterone, or in the presence of the female hormone estrogen, no pedicles will form, and neither will antlers develop later on, until after pedicles are formed. Due to some type of hormonal imbalance, buck fawns born late in the season, those poorly nourished during summer and autumn, or others that are subjected to severe social stress tend to grow small pedicles (or none at all) and invariably sprout undersized antlers a year later when one and a half years old.

In sharp contrast, some exceptionally well-nourished, physically superior buck fawns mature faster than normal. Whereas most bucks carry their first polished antlers when one and a half years old, some large male fawns may grow, polish, and shed small "buttons" (infant antlers less than half an inch long), thus undergoing one complete antler cycle prior to nine months of age. Males that exhibit such an advanced rate of maturity typically carry six- or eight-point racks as yearlings, instead of the spikes or forks more common for bucks their age.

In most whitetail populations, one female among every few thousand may also grow antlers. This phenomenon is usually due to some type of hormonal disturbance, a conclusion supported by the fact that does can also be experimentally induced to grow antlers if injected with testosterone. There is no consensus, however, whether female antlers are cast and replaced each year. Most doe antlers are unbranched structures that remain in velvet, but does with polished antlers have been reported.

Rapid growth in June and July is not limited to adult bucks' antlers. For whitetail fawns, also, summer is a period of rapid development in terms of size, coordination, and learning. Even the healthy two-week-old fawn is an amazingly energetic and agile little creature. It starts to exhibit playfulness and is capable of some tricky open-field running and long-distance travel when necessary. Such bursts of activity likely stimulate neuromuscular development and are necessary to build stamina and coordination. Although still essentially a "hider," the two-week-old fawn will likely flee rather than "freeze" when threatened, and once on its feet it can outmaneuver and outrun even the most athletic human.

Although fawn littermates occupy separate bedding sites during their first few weeks of life, they start bedding together, quite abruptly, when about 25 days old. Thereafter, they'll be found together most of the time. I've found some siblings together as young as 18 days, but others I've observed have not bedded together until they were 32 days old. Between twins and triplets, I've found no consistent difference in the age at which siblings first bed together.

The timing of sibling union seems to depend primarily upon the fawns' rate of physical and behavioral development. It's my impression that twins or triplets raised by prime-age does enjoy slightly better maternal nutrition, develop slightly more rapidly, and therefore start bedding together somewhat sooner than those reared by younger does.

After about one month of age, fawns more frequently initiate independent bouts of activity. They also become more visible at this time, and those that are in subpar health because of poor maternal nutrition, disease, or heavy parasitism become increasingly vulnerable to predation. In the Midwest, for example, young fawns are reasonably safe while hidden in dense vegetation, but slow, sickly animals from four to seven weeks old become more conspicuous and are easily picked off by marauding coyotes and domestic dogs.

Fawn "play" behavior, performed almost exclusively in the mother's presence, intensifies among healthy fawns more than one month old. Playful fawns may run circles around their mothers, jump and kick with their hind legs, and chase one another. But such frolicking decreases sharply by autumn, at which time fawns start to socialize and interact, oftentimes aggressively, with strange deer.

The lactating doe's extreme hostility towards other deer and her agonistic (aggressive

After being driven out of its mother's matriarchal group, a yearling buck will usually keep company with other yearling males under similar circumstances. However, yearling bucks may also try to associate with older-age bucks and buck groups. When they do, they are quickly introduced to the hierarchy of dominance that exists among older males, and sometimes those introductions are physical.

Whitetails consume a variety of summer's bounty, including grasses, forbs, agricultural crops and wild and domestic fruit. Apples are particularly relished by deer, and abandoned orchards anywhere in whitetail country will invariably be favored feeding areas.

or defensive interaction with other deer) territorial behavior associated with raising young diminishes after her offspring are four to six weeks old. Thereafter, she becomes much more tolerant of adult companionship and will probably expand her range to encompass more of that held by neighboring female relatives.

In the matriarchal social organization of female whitetails, daughters establish home ranges overlapping that of the dominant doe. When whitetails experience ideal range conditions and minimal predation, a high reproductive rate coupled with maximum longevity will permit the unhunted deer herd to increase annually at the rate of 50 to 60 percent. Multiple generations of females will thus come to inhabit a given area, and, in addition to the matriarch, her daughters, granddaughters, great-granddaughters, and even her great-great-granddaughters may become part of the social unit.

This system of female social organization presents a complex set of individual costs and benefits that have not been thoroughly investigated or evaluated. Theoretically, this organization evolved as a means of maximizing reproductive success during times of fluctuating availability of food resources, as undoubtedly occurred during pristine times, and it most certainly offers distinct anti-predator benefits. Even when deer densities are relatively high and keen competition for available space and resources occurs, the species' social order serves to minimize psychological tension and strife among individuals.

Depending upon her age and reproductive history, the matriarch's first late summer adult companions are likely to be yearling daughters and sons or, possibly, older daughters that occupy contiguous range but fail to raise young. Although considered to be the least gregarious of the genus *Odocoileus*, female whitetails do show, during times

Fawns often engage in play behavior during midsummer. These bursts of activity sometimes last for five to ten minutes and are initiated by one fawn running, bucking or kicking its hind legs in the air, which stimulates its sibling to similar behavior. Sometimes the fawns square off and attempt to butt one another or charge each other in what appears to be mock combat. As the young deer mature, these playful antics will become modified and incorporated in a repertoire of behaviors directed, often aggressively, toward other deer.

other than the fawning season, strong tendencies to form primary social groups composed of at least four to six animals. From all indications, it's the yearlings and non-productive two-year-old daughters, already predisposed to subordinate social roles, that "push" so persistently for this association and leadership, a tendency that is most pronounced when deer densities are high and during years of high newborn fawn mortality.

By the time fawns are eight weeks old, they will spend half their time traveling, feeding, and bedding with their mothers. Like her, too, they'll be most active around dawn, dusk, and at night, and will gradually integrate into complex social groups. It has been our experience in the Cusino enclosure investigations that newborn fawns are literally forced into association with older sisters sooner than ordinary when deer density is high and many young does fail to rear fawns. Under such circumstances, the ten-week-old fawn may be found associated with an adult female relative almost as often as it is with its mother.

Such socially compatible deer frequently greet one another by gently touching noses. Mutual grooming may follow. Mothers and fawns groom one another quite vigorously, particularly about the head and neck, but such behavior is common among all deer that associate on a regular basis. Even mature bucks will groom one another at times other

than the breeding season. In contrast, when deer enter into associations of questionable outcome, they timidly approach others of their species by avoiding direct eye contact and holding their ears back but pointing upward, a display of submissiveness.

Dominant-submissive relationships within a matriarchal group are closely related to female age, wherein older does consistently dominate the younger ones. Physical strength and individual behavioral traits may come more into play in competitive encounters between members of the same age class. But generally speaking, dominance hierarchy formation within a given kinship group comes about quite predictably and smoothly, with little serious conflict. Low-order non-contact aggressive threat displays or postures, such as the "ear-drop, hard-look" combination, "head-low threat," or "head-high threat," suffice to decide dominance in most confrontations among related females.

Beginning in late summer, however, much more violent conflicts may erupt between members of bordering kinship groups as deer become more active, range farther, and frequently clash in competition for choice foods at restricted locations. When vying for dominance, strange does more often employ "strikes," "chasing," "rearing," and "flails." And although whitetails normally aren't overly vocal, some older does well-seasoned in aggression may emit a forceful snort as they rush or lunge at an opponent.

Fawns lack aggressive experience but seem to catch on fast. They apparently learn a great deal by watching their mothers in action. After observing its mother challenge another deer, a fawn oftentimes attempts to repeat the threat by directing an initially feeble attack upon another fawn. This is learning by imitation. The young loser will frequently retreat to its mother's side, seeking maternal protection, whereas the victor will more likely look for another contender.

Among female whitetails, those reared by aggressive, socially high-ranking does like-wise tend to achieve high social status later in life, a direct result of their superior, learned aggressive behavior. By comparison, the male's social rank as a mature sire will hinge almost entirely upon his physical strength and degree of agonistic determination demonstrated in antler duels with other bucks. Large, strong males invariably attain higher dominance rank than smaller, weaker individuals.

In August, mature bucks, already well-rounded with fat and molting into their brown-gray winter coats, begin to appear in doe-occupied ranges. In twilight grazing associations the bucks seem to deliberately display themselves as they gently intermingle with slim red-coated does and their still-spotted but maturing fawns. Although the first does to breed are not likely to do so for another two months, bucks already appear well primed for the strenuous pre-rut activities that will commence within a few weeks. Lactating does and their fawns, on the other hand, are considerably delayed in such things as fattening and autumn coat change.

On northern range, as early as late August, increased testosterone secretion, cued to decreased photoperiod, arrests antler growth, hastens antler hardening (mineralization), and ultimately leads to velvet drying and stripping among some prime-age bucks. As with coat molt, those animals in superior health will complete the process first. Yearling bucks and other less-robust, older males will normally follow suit within a few weeks.

As summer fades to autumn, whitetail buck behavior begins to change. Physiologically, the males are rapidly approaching breeding readiness, and some prime-age individuals will already have stripped the velvet from their antlers and be displaying themselves to does. The annual contests that determine which bucks will dominate the breeding hierarchy will soon be at hand.

Most northern bucks will carry polished antlers by middle to late September, but those living in the South, in most instances, will be delayed by several weeks.

In late summer, before the first autumn frosts have singed the bracken, and despite the lush greenery that dominates the landscape, the premier appearances of prime-age bucks bearing glistening antlers hints strongly of coming events. Activities associated with the hectic autumn rut are close at hand. Summer, that tranquil, almost lazy time for the white-tailed deer, is over.

Autumn is a time of heightened activity in whitetail country. The rut has begun, and bucks, driven by hormonal influences to mate, spend much of their time engaged in breeding-related behavior. Does and yearling whitetails begin to behave differently now, too. The lethargic days of summer are over. In a very short time, before the end of autumn, the deer must accomplish their critical function of breeding and store life-sustaining fat reserves for the coming winter.

AUTUMN

Along with a fascinating array of associated behaviors, the whimsical months of autumn embrace the white-tailed deer's breeding season, its critical period of fattening, and the final stages of fawn growth. Fall is also the season of yearling male dispersal and, on occasion, the period when seasonal migration occurs in some northern areas.

In autumn, deer behavior tends to be complex — at times utterly baffling — and seems to change daily. Deer become extremely active, sometimes recklessly so, as though the animals were attempting to accomplish too much within a ridiculously limited time frame. This is especially true for deer living in northern regions where cold weather and heavy snowfall may occur early and restrict access to nutritious foods.

Because fat reserves can be metabolized for energy needs when forage is scarce, storing fat in autumn is a mechanism that enhances survival during the bleak winter months. Like other seasonal events in the white-tailed deer's life, the accumulation of fat is cued to photoperiod and is hormonally controlled. Also, it is an obligatory process, meaning that all deer are inclined to become fat in autumn. The whitetail's fat content in autumn — and therefore its chances for winter survival — will vary according to its diet, sex, age, and other factors.

In the annual physiological cycle of fattening, prime-age bucks achieve peak weights in early October, well before does and fawns. Does will require another month or more to accumulate fat reserves, and fawns, which must divert energy to physical growth as well as fat accumulation, may not reach optimal weights until December.

Because winter weather may arrive early across northern deer range, it's particularly important that fawns reach their full potential growth and lay away large amounts of fat as early as possible. Large fawns that are long-legged and fat have the best chance of surviving harsh winter weather and the food scarcity that invariably accompanies low temperatures, bitter cold winds, and snow cover.

Even poorly nourished fawns are physiologically compelled to store fat — if necessary, at the expense of additional skeletal growth. Therefore, well-nourished fawns will be structurally large as well as fat, whereas those fawns that subsist on diets of marginal quality may be fairly fat but usually have a noticeably smaller stature. Because fawns must simultaneously grow and fatten, however, they seldom achieve their maximum fat level until December, and because of this they are particularly sensitive to unfavorable weather and food shortages in autumn.

Adult does that have been stressed from lactating may not attain maximum fat levels before November. Others, those that have not been burdened by nursing fawns, experience less overall energy drain during summer and tend to fatten somewhat earlier. By comparison, prime-age bucks usually attain their peak seasonal body weight by early October or sooner, but those that are sexually active may metabolize 20 percent or more

of their fat reserves during the strenuous rut and will thus enter winter relatively lean.

As during other seasons, the whitetail's food habits in autumn vary according to the geographic region it inhabits, soil types, weather factors, and many other variables. Energy-rich foods high in carbohydrates, such as acorns, beechnuts, other starchy mast crops, as well as apples, cherries, grapes, and a host of other wild-growing and cultivated fruits, are choice deer foods in autumn because they promote fattening. Farm crops such as corn, soybeans, sugar beets, milo, rye, and winter wheat, whenever available, are also preferred by deer. In addition, cool weather and autumn rains stimulate a resurgent growth of nutritious forbs and succulent grasses that attract deer to feed in forest openings. Insufficient feed in autumn (due to mast crop failure, overgrazed range, early snowcover, or other variables) not only seriously impairs fawn growth rates and reduces fat accumulation among all deer, it also contributes to delayed breeding — hence late-born fawns the following spring — and, on average, fewer fawns are conceived per doe.

Among whitetails, loss of antler velvet signals the start of autumn and of rut-related activities. In most of North America the rut may span three to four months, usually starting in September and ending in January, but it may extend into February or even March in southern states. In the North, whitetails tend to breed earlier, but despite the prolonged period of rutting behavior demonstrated by prime-age bucks, the actual period of breeding is quite short. For example, in northern Michigan, where less than five percent of the doe fawns normally breed, 80 to 90 percent of the adult does breed in November, less than five percent breed in October, and most of the remainder breed in

December. By comparison, in southern Michigan and other areas of Midwest farmland where more than half of the doe fawns might achieve puberty and breed (mostly in December), the primary breeding period may extend a month longer. In Mississippi, breeding may span four or five months, with peak breeding activity occurring between mid-December and mid-January.

(Because deer living near the equator experience only slight seasonal changes in amount of daylight, they lack the photoperiod cues and thus the seasonal aspects of reproduction characteristic of their northern cousins. In the tropics, does may breed and give birth, and bucks may carry hardened antlers, at any time of the year.)

The rising levels of the male sex hormone testosterone that lead to antler maturation and velvet stripping also cause striking changes in buck behavior. However, the precise pattern and intensity of various rut-related activities will vary tremendously, depending upon buck age, herd density and composition, and other factors. For example, senior bucks — already well versed in agonistic behavior, scent marking, courtship finesse, and breeding — will display much more ritualistic rut behavior than younger bucks that have recently attained sexual maturity.

Another indication of the onset of autumn and rut-related behavior is reflected in whitetails' increased amount of social interactions. The white-tailed deer is not a highly gregarious species, but by no means is it an anti-social one. Whitetails regroup and socialize intensively immediately prior to the breeding season. Large numbers of deer — sometimes a hundred or so at a time — may congregate under cover of darkness in select open areas during September and October to graze and interact. Although it's generally assumed that these complex gatherings, which involve family groups as well as yearling and prime-age bucks, occur chiefly as responses to concentrations of nutritious forage, such behavior probably also serves other vitally important social functions.

I know of no investigation that has sought to deterime the psychological value of habitat "openness" to white-tailed deer. Nonetheless, I'm convinced that openings, while maybe not absolutely essential from a behavioral standpoint, serve deer a very special purpose in autumn. When interspersed throughout densely forested habitat, openings permit deer to gather, socialize, and visually communicate. Open areas void of predators serve as arenas where bucks can display, spar with one another, engage in serious fights to decide dominance, if necessary, and communicate their social status to prospective mates and competitors alike. Does and fawns, the wide-eyed spectators naturally drawn to such spectacular pre-rut exhibitions of male showmanship, seem to function as sentinels to warn the preoccupied males of approaching danger.

At this time of year, the behavior and status of yearling bucks differs greatly from that of the older bucks involved in these pre-rut activities. In spring, when they reach the age of one year, some whitetail males sever social ties with their mothers and other female

A yearling doe, her summer coat still evident but now being replaced by winter pelage, munches a fall-ripened apple. Building fat reserves in autumn is especially imperative for does, to sustain them and their fetuses through winter food shortages.

In fall, yearling bucks remaining with their mothers' matriarchal group will be harassed by the doe and her female relatives. The females may physically drive the sexually functional young bucks out of the group, forcing them to disperse to new range. This behavioral mechanism helps ensure healthy gene pools in whitetail herds.

kin. However, most year-old bucks still remain within familiar ancestral habitat during the summer and retain some contact with relatives. As the young male approaches sexual maturity at 16 to 17 months of age, though, he will be harassed, dominated, and rejected by his mother and older female relatives. He is automatically relegated to a lowly subordinate social position within the family group, and in all likelihood he would become a subdued "psychological castrate" if he remained with female kin during the rut.

Not surprisingly, then, just before breeding starts in autumn, most yearling males (80 percent or more) elect to disperse anywhere from two to 20 miles to new range, to areas where their breeding prospects are much improved. (Those males that do not disperse at yearling age generally do so when they are two and a half years old.)

It is "social pressure" then — or, more specifically, domination by female relatives, not breeding competition from other bucks — that is the primary stimulus prompting yearling males to disperse. Obviously, this phenomenon serves as a safeguard against inbreeding. As population density increases so does intra-family strife, which leads to even greater dispersal distance among yearling bucks. In autumn, therefore, yearling bucks are most appropriately referred to as "social floaters" because they are transient between female and male societies.

Why a dispersing buck eventually settles where he does is unknown. It seems reasonable, however, that his social acceptance by resident deer in the new area is a major factor. A young buck must achieve fraternal group membership, outlive his male companions, and engage in hierarchial competition over an extended period if he hopes to someday become a dominant breeder buck. Meanwhile, because relatively few dominant bucks do most of the breeding within an individual whitetail society, the yearlings must patiently serve an apprenticeship role, standing by but ready to take advantage should an unexpected breeding opportunity arise.

From an evolutionary standpoint, all bucks compete to individually produce as many offspring as possible. A buck's dominance rank, and therefore his chances of breeding, is highly dependent upon his body size and physical strength. The size of the buck's antlers, which serve as important display and fighting organs, and his aggressiveness, which is determined by the amount of testosterone coursing through his veins, are also important factors leading to attainment of dominance. All of these determinants increase with a buck's age and peak when he's between four and a half and eight and a half years old.

Initially, bucks "spar" in a highly ritualistic, almost congenial manner more reminiscent of a friendly handshake than true battle, and these early contests shouldn't be confused with serious "push-fights" which may occur later on in the rut. Yearling bucks, in particular, provoke antler contact with other bucks, which is probably an essential step in the complex and stormy social life of the young whitetail male. Prime-age bucks oftentimes tolerate the persistent and hyperactive yearlings and readily engage in grossly mismatched but gentle head-to-head scuffles with the youngsters — seemingly out of courtesy and more for show than anything else — at least during this early pre-breeding period. The middle-class bucks, generally those from two and a half to three and a half years old, seem to absorb much of this horseplay, thus somewhat buffering the alpha male — the buck with the highest dominance rank — from excessive, unnecessary energy drainage.

A sparring match often develops when one buck lowers his head and presents his antlers to another. The second buck usually accepts the challenge and engages his antlers with those of the challenger. The two bucks' antlers are then "clicked" together with minimal pushing and shoving by either contestant, and the match may end abruptly with no apparent winner or loser. Repeated bouts, which may each last for only a few seconds or could go on for minutes, are commonly interrupted with interludes of grazing. The amount of physical exertion involved in sparring increases as the season progresses. This allows bucks to gradually assess one another's strength with minimal injurious battle and establish a firm dominance hierarchy well in advance of the primary breeding season. Such social order minimizes unnecessary fighting, helps conserve energy until it is vitally needed, facilitates selective mating by physically superior sires, and

Although the timing of rut initiation varies according to latitude across the whitetail's range in North America, it phenologically begins when bucks begin to strip the velvet from their antlers. In the North this may occur as early as late August, and in the South as late as October.

assures genetic fitness within the herd.

The prime-age buck's behavior changes markedly as testosterone levels soar and peak, ordinarily in October. Male social tolerance then declines as big bucks adopt a noticeably belligerent attitude, become solitary travelers, and react violently to any intrusion of their guarded "personal space." And although the pesky yearlings may continue to spar among themselves during this primary breeding period, should they attempt such antics with an older buck at this time, they'll likely be met with a menacing ears-laid-back stare or a vicious charge.

By comparison, aggression among mature core members of cohesive fraternal groups is generally low in frequency and intensity, even when possession of a sexually receptive doe is at stake. Occasionally, however, two large, evenly matched, dominant bucks from bordering groups will encounter, and neither animal may willingly submit to low-level aggressive threats. An intense bout of hard shoving and neck twisting may then erupt, the participants sometimes charging forcefully at one another, tearing up the turf over a sizeable area. Only rarely does such fighting lead to fatal injuries or death, but broken antlers, gouged eyes, and torn ears are tell-tale signs of serious battle. Sometimes the combatants may even lock antlers. If bucks do become locked together and are unable to

The removal of antler velvet actually takes very little time. Most bucks, by rubbing their antlers on trees and shrubs, completely remove their velvet within a 24-hour period, and seeing a buck in the wild with bloody tissue dangling from its antlers is a very rare occurrence.
The buck on the facing page is orally stimulating itself, not an uncommon practice of rutting whitetail bucks, which sometimes also masturbate by rubbing their penis between their thighs.

free themselves, they eventually die from exhaustion or their inability to eat or drink.

In captivity, white-tailed bucks have lived to be more than 20 years old, but the odds are slim that any buck will attain a ripe old age in a wild, hunted population. Even in remote Upper Michigan, only one buck among every 3000 will likely live ten years. By comparison, only one in 360,000 bucks can be expected to last that long in the heavily hunted areas of northern Lower Michigan.

Nonetheless, should a dominant buck live long enough, he will ultimately lose his supreme status to a younger, stronger individual. Loss of dominance rank by an aged male probably signals his demise, as other bucks quickly detect his weakness, sense the opportunity to rise a notch on the hierarchial scale, and promptly challenge the old male's rank. The old buck is then met with repeated challenges at every turn, costing him precious energy and rapidly depleting his fat reserves. This, in turn, will leave him emaciated and vulnerable to death from malnutrition during the coming winter months. Most bucks that succumb in this fashion are eight to 12 years old.

Some interesting theories as well as a great deal of misinformation have been espoused

about the function of "buck rubs" and how they relate to the hierarchy structure among male whitetails. In the process of removing velvet, bucks naturally do some rubbing of trees and shrubs with their antlers. However, few "buck rubs" are made for that purpose, as velvet removal is normally completed within 24 hours. (It's actually quite rare to observe a buck in the wild with shredded velvet dangling from newly exposed blood-stained antlers.) And unlike roe deer or some other members of the deer family, white-tails rarely "mock fight" with trees. Instead, studies have revealed that most buck rubs are made by only a few dominant breeder bucks as a means of advertising their superior social rank.

Some highly enlightening research conducted at the University of Georgia by Drs. Thomas Atkeson and Larry Marchinton revealed that white-tailed deer possess specialized forehead scent glands, and that a buck will use secretions from these glands to mark its breeding range. Apparently, all deer have forehead glands that exhibit increased activity in autumn; however, as compared to younger males and females, socially high-ranking bucks exude greater amounts of the glandular material. Because bucks rub primarily with their antler base and forehead, each blaze created by rubbing also carries the maker's scent — and pheromones, or chemical signals, which convey specific information concerning the maker's identity as well as other personal messages. In other words, each antler rub serves as the dominant buck's sign-post, his special calling card notifying other deer in the area of his eminent presence.

Antler rubbing is definitely keyed to rising levels of testosterone, which also precipitates aggressive behavior and dominance attainment. Bucks that are "winners" — those with socially recognized high rank — become psychologically and physiologically stimulated due to increased testosterone production and are driven to advertise themselves through frequent scent marking. It seems only reasonable to assume that habitual "losers" suffer the opposite, depressing effects. Dominant bucks will continue to antler-rub as long as they carry mature, hardened antlers. In fact, a highly stimulated buck may continue to rub-mark with his forehead after casting his antlers.

Well established dominant whitetail bucks maintain year-round supremacy over their peers and control a stable male society within a given area. They do not establish individual breeding territories, in the strict definition of that term, but their fresh antler rubs serve as sign-posts to inform all other deer that they're "number one" in the area. The dominant male's companions freely travel this marked range and do some rub-marking themselves, but they heed their leader's posted warnings and behave sub-missively whenever he's in the vicinity.

Soon after "rubbing out," rut-experienced bucks start to wander extensively, shifting their centers of activity to interact with other deer over a potentially large breeding range of anywhere from one to four or five square miles. They tend to travel a larger autumn range when deer density is low, whereas they're apt to cover less area when deer are

Common sights in whitetail country each fall are rubbed trees and ground scrapes.
They indicate that rutting bucks are in the vicinity, and their frequency and dates of
initiation indicate the number and age of the bucks that make them.

A freshly pawed ground scrape is indicated by a roughly circular area in which ground duff and vegetation has been dug away, revealing the loose, underlying soil. The buck making the scrape urinates on it, creating a sign-post that attracts does and indicates his presence to other bucks.

plentiful. Also, they begin rub-marking their domain almost immediately, without much prior testing or combat. By comparison, young bucks have little status or rank to advertise — even in the absence of mature bucks — until they seriously compete with one another and dominant individuals of their age group emerge, which isn't likely to occur until late October.

The seasonal pattern and frequency of buck rubs, therefore, provides considerable insight into the age composition and social stability of bucks inhabiting a given area. Yearling bucks, on average, make less than half as many total rubs during a season as prime-age individuals. An increased frequency of antler rubbing in September, then, will

invariably indicate the presence of an older buck. In contrast, greatly delayed and less frequent rubbing is more prevalent in heavily hunted deer herds in which few males survive to maturity.

When in the mood, bucks rub just about anything with their antlers, including fence posts and powerline poles, but they seem to prefer soft-barked saplings of aspen, red maple, dogwood, and alder. (In one Georgia study, bucks rubbed 47 of 58 available tree species.) They rarely rub the same stem on return visits but will more likely rub another nearby, and will rub with increasing vigor as the rut progresses, exposing more of the inner bark and generating larger, more-visible rub marks during peak rut. Roughly five percent of buck-rubbed trees, generally those located at strategic locations of heavy deer travel, will be re-rubbed in successive years.

One October evening, my wife, Janice, and I tested the visual response of deer to artificial buck rubs in the Cusino enclosure, a mile square in area. I'd cut several one-to two-inch diameter aspen saplings from outside the area, scraped them to resemble buck rubs, and stuck them into the ground within view of our separate blinds.

Sign-posting the scrape site involves the deposition of a number of glandular substances including scent from the buck's interdigital glands; its tarsal glands, on which it urinates; and its forehead glands, which are used to scent mark overhead limbs found at the majority of scrape sites.

During the evening watch, all of the dozen or so does and fawns that came near my "dummy" rub stopped to investigate. One doe seemed particularly puzzled. She made three repeat visits, each time intently sniffing the stem in an apparent attempt to identify the odor of the mysterious rub maker. I was disappointed, however, when a couple of nice bucks passed by without so much as a side glance at the fake rub.

Jan's observations went much the same, at least until the area's "number-two" buck came on the scene. "He went straight to the fake rub," Jan reported later, "sniffed it only briefly, then lowered his head and really leaned into it."

Unfortunately, the stem was not dug-in firmly and it toppled to the ground after only a couple of strokes of the buck's antlers. "He just stood there awhile," according to Jan, "then calmly walked away as if nothing had happened."

This one simple experiment rather clearly demonstrates that deer, regardless of sex or age, respond to such visual stimuli and respond inquisitively to anything closely resem-

*The complex of behaviors involved in scent-marking are, at best, little understood.
The chemistry and behavioral and physiological mechanisms involved, which may vary from one
area of whitetail habitat to another, are the subject of considerable controversy.*

bling a freshly made buck rub. Close follow-up inspection then permits them to identify and learn more about the maker, based upon the odor of forehead scent deposited on the blaze.

The "buck scrape" is another form of sign-posting. Scrapes, made by white-tailed

[89]

bucks primarily during the courtship and breeding period (although I've found some made in May, and others suggest that summertime scraping does occur), appear to serve two distinct purposes, one being to attract breeding females, and the other to intimidate rival males. The typical scrape is an area two to three feet in diameter where a buck has pawed away the surface duff to bare soil and then urinated. A scent-marked tree limb extends over the top of 80 to 90 percent of all scrape sites.

Regardless of the type of scent mark involved — rub or scrape — the general rule is that the dominant animal is the message "sender," while the subordinate is the "receiver." However, on rare occasions even does apparently make scrapes, and, surprisingly, at times other than the rut. Females reportedly urine-mark their newly formed scrapes, but to my knowledge they have never been known to freshen them nor to scent-mark an overhead limb in conjunction with the scrape. The social significance, if any, of the female's "pseudo" scrape is unknown.

While most buck rubs are found in dense sapling growth, most scrapes occur where the understory is open. Bucks seem to purposely cluster their scrapes where they'll draw the greatest attention from neighboring deer, and often locate scrapes where re-grouped females concentrate their bedding and feeding activities. Lines of scrapes are sometimes found along routes between these sites.

It is assumed that does attracted to a freshly scented buck scrape will urinate near it. Presumably the tending buck then readily detects, through the urine's odor, those does in estrus, and can then easily scent-trail them for breeding; however, solid scientific evidence corroborating this behavior is not yet available.

In the process of pawing the scrape, the buck naturally deposits some scent from the interdigital glands located between his toes. Usually, he will also urinate on the scrape, in a crouched position, allowing the urine to flow over his tarsal glands, located hock-high on the inside surface of his hind legs. While urinating, the buck rubs his hind legs, and thus his tarsal glands, together. This is referred to as "rub-urination," a behavior also exhibited by does and fawns (for unknown reasons) throughout the year. During the rut, the tarsal glands of dominant bucks show heavy staining from frequent rub-urination, a practice which also produces a pungent, musky odor that may be detected at considerable distances even by humans.

Ground-deposited scents are unquestionably an important component of any buck scrape. The scents provide important clues to the maker's identity, breeding readiness, and no doubt relay other vital messages — possibly, as some investigators have proposed, even the maker's health status. The truly mystifying feature of any heavily used buck scrape, however, is the scent-marked overhead limb — sometimes referred to as the "licking branch" — which extends about head high directly above the pawed site. This may be a single slender stem or consist of a clump of bushy multi-branched stems. In

Some observers of deer behavior believe scrapes serve as dominance areas, or small breeding territories for dominant bucks. But other observers have witnessed subordinate bucks freshening scrapes of dominant bucks and have seen yearling bucks roll in dominant males' scrapes, which would seem to refute the contention that scrapes serve territorial functions.

Early in the rut, sparring is often of low intensity and serves the purpose of establishing the dominance hierarchy among bucks. Sparring between young bucks is more frequent than between older males, but young bucks may also provoke older males into gentle "shoving matches." Later in the rut, juvenile provocations of older bucks are not tolerated, and when evenly matched dominant bucks encounter one another, serious fighting may ensue.

either case, the scent-marked twigs always possess dry, broken tips, which probably enhance their scent-holding properties. Bucks accomplish this limb-tip conditioning either by thrashing the stems with their antlers or by biting off the stems' terminal buds. (While doing so, scent from a buck's forehead glands is quite likely deposited on the stems, accidentally or purposely.) Pieces of branches found lying in scrapes clearly attest to these more-vigorous types of marking episodes.

When the overhead limb consists of little more than a single thin stem, the buck rubs more gently, carefully guiding the stem's feathered tip back and forth along the side of his face, beginning at the base of the nostril. When doing so, he stands as if in a trance, outstretched, as if meticulously and delicately anointing the fragile twig with some magical ingredient, stopping periodically to sniff and check his scenting progress.

For many years, the whitetail's preorbital glands, which have ducts opening near the corner of each eye, were thought to be the primary scent producers for marking overhead limbs at scrapes. In whitetails, though, this gland seems to serve principally as a tear duct; there is no evidence that it functions as an important pheromone producer.

Some hunters and biologists contend that a buck's licking and muzzle rubbing of its

tarsal glands may allow for later transfer of scent from that gland to the overhanging limb. Observations generally show, however, that large male whitetails infrequently lick their tarsal glands during the rut.

Another plausible explanation is that white-tailed bucks scent-mark scrape limbs with secretions from nasal subaceous glands — newly discovered glands found inside each nostril in white-tailed deer. According to Drs. Atkeson and Marchinton, this gland, which occurs in other ungulate species as well, serves an unknown function. Based on evidence produced by these researchers, however, in conjunction with observations of the white-tailed buck's limb-marking tactics at scrapes, the nasal gland could serve as an important pheromone producer for rutting bucks and might serve other communicative functions, even for females, during other seasons as well.

Scrape making is an instinctive behavior among whitetail bucks, but it appears to improve with experience. In the Cusino enclosure, where we could closely regulate buck age composition, individual yearling bucks made only about 15 percent as many total scrapes as those made by prime-age bucks, even when all older bucks were purposely eliminated from the herd. Furthermore, prime-age bucks usually started low-level scraping in September, whereas yearlings made no scrapes until mid-October, or about two weeks before the first doe bred. Regardless of the ages of bucks (or does) involved in these studies, scrape making and tending consistently peaked for a two-week period in late October and early November, about two weeks before peak breeding, then dropped off sharply and ceased entirely by mid-December, by which time nearly all does had bred and snow cover stood a foot or more deep in this northern region.

Even individual prime-age bucks vary tremendously in their scrape-making ability (or motivation); some may make hundreds of scrapes during the course of a rut season, whereas others might make only a few dozen. Such variations in performance may be attributed to differences in herd density, amount of breeding competition, food distribution, or other, unknown factors.

Few scrapes show repeated pawing for extended periods. Even those sites that are worked-over repeatedly for five or six consecutive days are oftentimes ignored, for whatever reason, for days or weeks, only to show a resurgence of late season use. On average, prime-age bucks only freshen and maintain slightly more than half of the scrapes they make, versus about a 40 percent retreatment rate for yearling bucks. Given reasonably stable habitat and deer populations, though, certain scrapes may show use for generations. (Nearly half of 150 scrapes I examined in the Cusino enclosure in 1977 were also used in 1978.) Aside from being located in areas of heavy deer use with open understories, these high-use sites tend to be located on easily bared soil, and all possess the critically important overhead limb.

As mentioned earlier, white-tailed bucks are not considered to be territorial because

Combat between prime-age bucks serves an ecological function by determining which bucks will attain reproductive rights, thus ensuring the genes of physically superior male whitetails will be maintained in the herd's gene pool.

Buck fights can result in eye injuries, broken antler tips, or total antler loss.
The buck above probably received an antler tip to its eye during such a match of
strength. On the following spread, a buck displays a blood-stained antler tip after using his
rack to prod a reluctant doe, goring her udder in the process.

they permit male associates to travel the same breeding range. Nonetheless, some researchers and hunters contend that buck scrapes serve as dominance areas — "mini" breeding areas, so to speak — where the scrape maker enjoys a higher dominance rank than he might otherwise hold at some other location. Supporting evidence indicates that subordinate bucks sometimes behave cautiously while in the vicinity of a dominant buck's scrape or that they may avoid these sites altogether. In other instances, however, yearling bucks have been observed to roll in the scrape made by a dominant individual, and I've witnessed several different prime-age bucks freshening the same scrape at different times, which seems to run contrary to the "scrape territory" theory.

Otherwise, scent communication among whitetails, particularly as it relates to scrap-

ing behavior, remains largely a mystery. The concept is highly complex and controversial. The exact chemistry, behavior, and physiological mechanisms involved are poorly understood and, likely, vary greatly from one area to the next, depending on herd density and age-sex composition, habitat characteristics, and other, unidentified factors.

About the time that bucks become solitary travelers and scraping activity dramatically escalates, they start to chase does in earnest, testing them for breeding receptiveness. This sudden change in behavior, which occurs only a few weeks before the first females breed, is probably triggered by increased production of testosterone in males, in addition to seasonal changes in female scent and behavior. The exact role that "biostimulation" — certain potent and mysterious olfactory, auditory, visual, and tactile stimuli — plays in stimulating the sexes and synchronizing breeding is unknown. It's interesting to note, however, that close and unnatural confinement of bucks with does in small pens prior to the rut can stimulate females and advance their breeding date by eight to ten days.

Doe fawns usually achieve puberty and breed only under the most favorable circum-

To determine a doe's stage of estrus, a rutting buck will taste and smell a spot where a doe has urinated, and oftentimes the buck will perform a lip-curl, or "flemen," while inhaling the scent. If he determines the doe is possibly ready for mating, he will scent-trail her, employing short choppy steps, holding his head low and his neck outstretched while approaching her.

stances of excellent nutrition and low herd density, but even yearling does are extremely "stress" sensitive and may fail to breed if subjected to nutritional shortage prior to the rut. Young does (fawns and yearlings), as well as malnourished adults, compared to well-fed prime-age individuals, typically breed later and conceive fewer fawns and a lower proportion of female fetuses.

Once breeding starts, prime-age bucks become extremely active. They travel from one doe group to the next within their established range in constant search of receptive females. The rutting buck rests only briefly, feeds very little, and loses considerable body weight within relatively few weeks time.

The doe also shows a dramatic rise in movement activity (about 28 times normal) with the onset of estrus, which is coincident with increased ovarian production of estrogen, the female hormone that precipitates a doe's mating urge. In one instance we calculated that a penned doe walked over 20 miles the night prior to mating. In the wild, such wanderings would be adaptive in that they'd increase a doe's chances of finding a mate if one were not already in close attendance.

A doe will accept a male only during peak estrus, which lasts about 24 hours. If she is not bred or does not become pregnant, the cycle may recur in three to four weeks. Thereafter, if she remains in peak physical condition but does not become pregnant, she might recycle several more times. Unless sexually mature males are in extremely short supply — a major concern only where intensive hunter harvesting of antlered bucks precedes the primary breeding period — most does likely breed in their first estrus. This is critically important on northern range, where it is essential that fawns be born "on schedule" in spring to permit maximum growth and development prior to winter.

When a buck finds a doe ready to mate, the pair will isolate themselves from other deer and spend from one to two days in each other's company, during which time they may copulate several times.

Does do not allow bucks to approach them closely prior to the time of mating. Instead, the male scent-trails the female, following some distance behind. Although overly energetic young bucks may wildly chase does once visual contact with them is made, older bucks experienced in courtship and breeding are more inclined to test the receptivity of does in a highly ritualized fashion. The prime-age buck will trot in short, choppy steps toward the doe, hold his neck outstretched and his head low to the ground while keeping his muzzle slightly elevated. He may simultaneously grunt or emit a sort of wheeze-snort as he exhales through his flared nostrils. The apparent purpose of such behavior is to encourage the female to urinate so that the buck can then determine, through the doe's urine odor, if she is approaching estrus. In some cases the doe will circle the buck or run back and forth in front of him before urinating, which seems to gain his attention and reflect her favorable response toward the buck as a potential mate.

The buck will then sniff the doe's urine or taste it, apparently testing it to determine her stage of estrus, and he will oftentimes perform a lip-curl, or "flehmen." In doing so, he holds his neck and chin upward at about a 45-degree angle while curling back his upper lip and inhaling. This response might only last for five to ten seconds, during

which time the buck apparently decides whether the doe is approaching estrus and worth pursuing.

Once a buck locates a doe in estrus that is willing to stand for copulation, he stays close and tends her carefully. The pair generally isolate themselves from all other deer; the doe may even willingly leave or be driven from her normal home range during her brief period of peak estrus. The pair-bond breeding system, as normally occurs among forest-dwelling whitetails, reportedly differs considerably from that of deer inhabiting the open savannah grasslands of Texas, where bucks show a tendency toward a harem-type breeding behavior, wherein each dominant buck attempts to control a group of does.

The breeding pair may mate several times during their bonding period, but there is no good information available as to how long they remain together. It's been my observation that a dominant buck remains with a particular doe only a day or two. Because breeding rights among males are determined by dominance, however, a subordinate buck that finds a receptive doe and successfully mates with her may still be driven away if a more-dominant buck happens along.

Whether female whitetails show preference for mates that possess superior traits — and solicit their attention, as some evolution theorists propose — has not been proven. In theory, the doe that "chooses" to mate with a large-bodied, large-antlered buck selects an individual possessing superior hereditary traits, thus assuring thrifty progeny and the perpetuation of genetic fitness within the herd. Certainly the evidence that females avoid the sexual advances of young, related, reproductively active males lends some support to the "mate preference" theory. Likewise, one might speculate that the prime-age buck's elaborate scent-marking system may even permit a doe to visit the scrapes made by a particular male, where she might deposit her estrous scent to draw the attention of that buck. By comparison, young bucks inexperienced in rut-related behavior may be very capable breeders when the opportunity arises, but their "seek-and-chase" courtship style likely eliminates any chances of selective breeding. These facets of the whitetail's breeding behavior are obviously poorly understood and deserve further in-depth study. The findings could have profound effects on deer management philosophy and future harvest strategies.

Although fall weather may be relatively prolonged in the South, autumn on northern deer range is an unpredictable season that may switch to winterlike conditions overnight. Along Lake Superior, for instance, subzero temperatures and heavy snowfall are not at all unusual in November, and such harsh conditions are normally expected to occur in December.

In winter, low temperatures and cold winds accelerate whitetails' body heat loss, and even scant snowcover can force them to shift from grazing on nutritious herbaceous forage to consuming less-nourishing, woody browse. This combination of a low-quality diet and excessive body heat loss may put deer on a negative energy balance, meaning that more calories are burned for basic body needs than are assimilated from the food the deer consume. This abrupt switch in metabolism, when it occurs, can interrupt breeding. On northern range these interruptions account for infrequent breeding of doe fawns

All does do not come into estrus simultaneously in a given range, and mating in
northern latitudes often extends into the months when snow covers the ground.
Late copulations such as these, usually between dominant bucks and yearling does
or doe fawns, produce fawns that are born late the following spring.

and, on occasion, the high incidence of barren yearlings.

The timing, magnitude, and duration of such weather-related hardships naturally varies from north to south, as does the whitetail's response. But regardless of when such metabolic stress sets in, thereafter, deer can no longer afford their frivolous and energetic autumn lifestyle. They must adjust to environmental conditions and minimize energy expenditures. Otherwise, they will perish.

The white-tailed deer's dense insulating winter coat and ability to store fat in autumn are important adaptations that enhance the species prospects for survival during the crucial winter period. Additionally, whitetails have evolved some intriguing seasonal adjustments in physiology and behavior that allow them to conserve energy, evade predators, and survive winter against what at times appears to be overwhelming odds. In recent years, biologists have come to better understand how whitetails adjust to seasonal changes and manage to survive the stressful winter period — and why they sometimes fail.

*Winter in whitetail country, especially in northern range,
is a time of trying circumstances. Harsh energy-depleting weather
and food shortages will take a toll on the herd before the spring
thaw. How many deer will die depends on a number of factors,
including herd density, temperatures, snow depth,
and the duration of severe weather.*

WINTER

The winter of 1964-65, my first at Cusino, was one of prolonged and relentless severity in Upper Michigan. I'm certain there have been more severe winters, but that one was my introduction to the wintering whitetail's way of life and death along Lake Superior, where the harsh winter environment seems far better suited to moose than to deer.

A raging mid-November blizzard drove deer from the surrounding uplands into the Petrel Grade deer yard (an area of conifer swampland that I studied in eastern Alger County) early that year, and continued heavy snowfall locked them tightly, sooner than usual, in core areas that provided prime shelter but little food. I began to find starved fawns in February, and by late March even prime-age does were dying from malnutrition. More than 140 whitetails died that winter in my one-square-mile study area; the survivors did not start leaving the area until mid-April.

The high death rate was not at all surprising, of course, considering the deer had been subjected to five long months of bitter cold, deep snow, and limited food supplies in the browsed-out swamp. What surprised me was to see so many deer somehow survive. At the time, I considered the animal's hardiness remarkable and downright mysterious. Since then, researchers including myself have gained considerable insight into the adaptations of white-tailed deer to winter stress, but I will always be greatly impressed by the

[113]

Physiologically, white-tailed deer are adapted to cold weather. Their insulating coat of hollow hairs helps retain the animals' body heat and will simultaneously keep snow from melting on the coat's exterior, thus keeping the deer dry and warm.

species' ability to survive such unbelievable hardship at the northern edge of their geographic range.

When winter begins, deer have not yet adjusted physiologically and behaviorally to withstand cold weather and the associated diet change. They respond rather sensitively to early winter climatic stress by becoming more active, eating more, and seeking shelter. Southern whitetails seldom lack adequate cover and can usually find relief from adverse weather within their normal home range. In the north, however, protective conifer cover becomes critically important as deer vacate vast areas of summer range and travel considerable distances to reach their traditional wintering grounds.

This inherent, so-called "yarding," behavior demonstrated by northern whitetails likely evolved as an energy-conserving and predator defense adaptation for winter survival. Historically, deer that responded in such a manner survived to reproduce and perpetuate this trait. Those that did not adapt died. In a sense, sufficient food became a secondary consideration for northern whitetails faced with cold weather and deep snow. Nonetheless, the amount of good-quality food available to them invariably determines how many deer can survive the stressful winter season.

Low temperatures and cold winds are the principal factors causing high rates of body heat loss. Combined, these climatic influences prompt northern deer to shift from scattered distribution on summer range to highly concentrated numbers in preferred areas of dense conifer cover. Nothing is more effective in motivating deer to migrate than a full-

scale blizzard, but rather dramatic shifts in deer distribution sometimes do occur during very cold, windy weather in November and December, even when snow cover may only be light. Increasing snow depths may restrict deer movements once they are in the yarding area, but major migrations take place before deep snow poses a serious hinderance to deer travel.

Northern whitetails possess a strong homing instinct and usually return to the same wintering area each year. If temperatures should moderate during early winter, and snow is not too deep, deer may return temporarily to their summer range. This means that whitetails sometimes make several migratory trips before settling in their chosen winter habitat. Most deer travel five to ten miles from summer to winter range, but a host of factors may influence their migratory distance. Generally speaking, however, those living where the topography is relatively flat tend to travel somewhat farther than those that occupy hilly country. Even in Michigan's Upper Peninsula, for example, studies have revealed that deer living in the eastern half of the peninsula, where the terrain is gently rolling, travel significantly farther, on average, to reach their winter yards than do those deer living in the peninsula's rugged and hilly western half (9.3 versus 7.5 miles, respectively).

Because related does and fawns band together in autumn, fawns likely learn lengthy migratory routes from their mothers, aunts, or older sisters. This doe-fawn social bond is particularly important in winter because such behavior increases the young animals' chances of finding "tried and tested" winter habitat and provides them the additional safety inherent in group associations.

Whether northern bucks migrate to winter yards with other deer or migrate alone, to

Early winter presents little problem for whitetails. As long as snow is
only moderately deep, their behavior seems little changed from that of fall.
In fact, the breeding season is usually still in progress at this time. If temperatures
drop and snow accumulates to appreciable depths, however, significant
number of deer in northern ranges will begin to migrate to winter yarding areas.

my knowledge, is unknown. Once in the wintering area, however, members of fraternal groups likely reunite and spend the winter together, just as they do in non-migratory herds. Also, no investigations I know of have dealt solely with the migratory behavior of dominant breeder bucks. One might logically assume, however, that a dominant buck would remain on his breeding range and not migrate until after the last doe has left. How a buck behaves when an estrous doe decides to leave his range, or when another passes through on her way to the winter yard, is anyone's guess. Should one dominant buck trespass upon another's breeding range in search of or accompanied by an estrous doe, however, a serious battle between the still-antlered bucks can be expected.

In the North, where bucks generally cast (drop) antlers from mid-December to late January, some bucks cast their antlers while still on summer range, others carry them into wintering areas. Also, older, larger, and more-dominant bucks tend to cast antlers earlier than young, small subordinates. By comparison, in Mississippi and Georgia some bucks may retain antlers until March or April, and large-antlered bucks there reportedly carry antlers later than small-antlered ones.

A buck may drop both of his antlers on the same day, possibly only minutes apart, or, more rarely, carry one antler a week or more longer than the other. Presumably it is the decrease in production of testosterone that is responsible for antler casting. It is important to note, however, that it is not latitude per se that causes the north-to-south difference in antler casting periodicity. The buck's nutrition and general health status, as well as his

dominance rank, directly influence testosterone production and, subsequently, antler retention. We demonstrated, for example, that artificially raising the nutritional level of our enclosed herd at Cusino (via supplemental feeding) greatly delayed antler casting and caused many bucks to carry their antlers until March or, in a few instances, even April. Improved nutrition for our northern bucks, then, produced an antler casting schedule more closely resembling that of southern whitetails.

Conifer swamps in northern states may attract densities of several hundred deer per square mile in winter, but dense stands of hemlock, jackpine, spruce, balsam, and other conifer types may also support wintering deer herds where the weather isn't too severe. Under natural conditions, however, no single habitat provides deer with maximum protection from cold windy weather and also provides adequate food supplies.

Average temperatures differ by only a few degrees among niches of a deer yard, but the amount of wind action and resulting air chill (convective heat loss) varies tremendously. Dense stands of 60 to 80 year old swamp conifers dominated by northern white cedar provide the best shelter. Conifer swamps have the narrowest thermal range and exhibit five to 200 times less wind flow as compared to other types of winter habitat. The trees' tight canopy also intercepts much of the snowfall, and ground level accumulations of snow pack more firmly, making travel easier. A notable disadvantage of such cover, of course, is that very little browse grows in the shaded understory.

The ideal conifer deer yard in the northern Great Lakes region, therefore, consists of blocks of mature dense swamp conifers adjacent to young food-producing stands of northern white cedar, an unexcelled winter deer browse. Unfortunately, such ideal circumstances rarely exist today because most cedar stands have been overbrowsed by deer or have grown out of their reach through natural pruning.

Few if any white cedar swamps are currently being cut and managed specifically to rehabilitate them as deer wintering areas. On private lands, cutting of white cedar often proceeds with little or no regard for the future well-being of deer. Meanwhile, largely because game managers disagree among themselves as to the proper procedures that should be employed, or because they fear intensive browsing at present day high deer densities will preclude any chance of re-establishing the highly preferred cedar in cutover areas, many biologists oppose logging of deer yards on public lands. Without proper management, however, even uncut stands will eventually become overmature and progress from even- to uneven-age structure, which will greatly diminish their thermal cover value.

In early winter, healthy deer readily travel a mile or so from favored resting sites to feed most heavily around sunrise, midday, sunset, and twice at night. They're normally most inactive for a period of two or three hours starting about an hour after sunset.

During their initial adjustment to winter weather, deer undergo certain physiological changes, including reduced thyroid function and decreased metabolic activity, meaning, of course, that less food is thereafter required to maintain basic body functions. By midwinter, whitetails gear down to what might be considered a torpid or semi-hibernating state and become quite resistant to nutritional deprivation and climatic stress. They voluntarily reduce their food intake by about 30 percent, regardless of the quality or amount of food available, and they decrease their movement activity by at least 50 percent. These adaptive tactics enable them to minimize wasteful expenditures of energy, rely heavily on fat stores during adverse periods, and coexist in a crowded, hostile environment.

When severely stressed by deep snow, cold weather, and poor food conditions, deer may restrict their activity to less than 80 acres of choice cover and spend much of their time bedded. Although the whitetail's winter coat — comprising fine "underfur" and long, hollow outer hair — provides excellent insulation, browse-nourished animals, in particular, carefully select wintertime bed sites to minimize body heat loss. They choose beds with good overhead cover, thus reducing radiant emission to clear cold skies and reducing convective heat loss during cold, windy periods. On warm sunny days they prefer open sunlit beds on south-facing slopes, to benefit as much as possible from incoming solar radiation.

Once acclimated to their chosen winter habitat, white-tailed deer can become extremely stubborn and reluctant to explore or deviate from their established daily routine. They will be most active during the warmer daytime hours, travel a network of firmly

The onset of winter does not interrupt the breeding activities of dominant breeder bucks. As long as testosterone levels in these males remain high, they will continue to exhibit aggressive behavior toward other bucks, driving them away from does within the dominant bucks' breeding range.

Besides weather-related stress on whitetails in winter, predation and other mortality factors persist or become more severe. Although reduced movement of deer in winter may reduce mortality due to road accidents and other miscellaneous factors, carnivorous predation usually increases, and packs of dogs chasing deer become serious problems for whitetails in some locations.

packed trails when snow is deep, and may refuse to travel more than a few hundred feet from protective cover to feed. It's as though the stressed animal possesses its own sophisticated computer system necessary to calculate energy cost-benefit ratios, predict potential predator risks, and make the best judgments possible in order to stay alive.

Nonetheless, from an energy standpoint, yarding is not absolutely necessary in order for whitetails to survive cold temperatures. Even in northern Minnesota deer withstand subzero temperatures while feeding on corn and bedding in open fields. The high-energy diet of corn, along with some browse, apparently provides these deer with a balanced diet and enough energy to compensate for metabolic heat loss. Although such whitetail habits are becoming increasingly common in northern states — as are some wintering deer herds becoming dependent upon artificial feeding handouts — if such food sources become limited, for whatever reason, deer so exposed to cold weather will likely experience a serious energy deficit and dire consequences can be expected.

Even fawns semi-starved in autumn can survive winter if good-quality food is readily available, as these undersized animals tend to eat more in winter, utilize their food more efficiently, and conserve energy by being extremely inactive. Unfortunately, however, this type of sharply contrasting nutritional pattern — scant resources in autumn but superb in winter — seldom occurs naturally on northern deer range, and few fawns so stunted normally manage to survive severe winters.

In winter, food availability is naturally diminished, and in forested hardwood areas, particularly, deer then browse only on low-nutrient foods. Such poor-quality edibles as bark, buds, and lichens compose only a subsistence diet, however, and during a prolonged winter may not be enough to keep whitetails healthy and able to fend off stress-related diseases and starvation. When food shortages are especially severe, whitetails will sometimes fight over food, flailing or kicking at other deer to drive them away from a source of nourishment.

White-tailed deer are ruminants with a typical compound stomach (rumen, reticulum, omasum, and abomasum). Thus they can meet their energy needs directly from nutrients consumed in food plus those synthesized by micro-organisms in the rumen and reticulum.

Commonly referred to as "browsers" because they feed on tender buds, twigs, leaves,

A buck digs through a thin blanket of snow for acorns. When snow depths become greater, however, the amount of energy a whitetail expends uncovering foodstuffs on the ground or travelling appreciable distances to forage may be more than the sustenance returns, creating a negative energy balance. This is when the animals' fat reserves become critical to their overwinter survival, and it is the time when deer with insufficient reserves, and those that are old, sick, or otherwise infirm may, in a sense of costs in the natural world, pay their final debt.

and needles of certain trees and shrubs, whitetails are not "super ruminants" and can not digest some species of woody browse. Actually, whitetails prefer to graze on herbaceous forage that is richer in protein, calcium, and phosphorous and is easily digested for energy needs. Also, they will readily supplement their diet with energy-rich fruits, nuts (acorns are a widespread natural food especially high in fat content and energy; normally an important autumn food, whitetails will dig through considerable snow to feed on them), and nourishing farm crops, switching to less nutritious woody browse only when necessary.

In the Great Lakes region, northern white cedar is about the only woody browse that, by itself (three to six pounds per deer per day), will sustain deer through a 100-day plus yarding season. Other species of low nutritive value, such as hemlock, maple, ash, aspen, birch, dogwood, among other tree and shrub species, may suffice only when available in great variety and abundance or when consumed along with more energy-rich foods. Deer that starve frequently have rumens filled with balsam, spruce, alder, pine, and other poorly digestible material.

During winter, timber cuttings conducted in the vicinity of overgrown and browsed-out deer yards commonly attract large concentrations of deer that feed upon the felled browse. Because the welfare of northern deer depends heavily upon their nutritional status in winter, these operations can be highly beneficial to deer, as an abundant supply of browse in close proximity to protective cover allows deer to minimize energy expenditures when traveling from resting sites to feeding locations. As a result, when carefully planned and conducted, winter cuttings can permit far more deer to survive than the habitat might otherwise naturally produce or support.

Frequently, however, winter timber-harvesting operations are inadequate for deer either because the browse provided is of poor quality or limited in quantity. Additionally, large concentrations of deer attracted to cuttings in early winter are often left stranded when logging operations cease in late winter, just when deer have the greatest need for the browse.

If high-quality food is concentrated and limited, considerable social strife, which equates to wasted energy, can develop as hungry deer fight over whatever meager amounts of good food are available. A strict dominance hierarchy, or "peck order," develops wherein deer come to recognize one another and each quickly learns its respective rank. As a result, although the whitetail's level of social intolerance tends to increase due to hunger as winter progresses, the intensity of deer combat usually diminishes in most late winter conflicts.

The older, larger, and more-aggressive animals typically dominate the younger, smaller ones, and the most dominant individuals invariably gain a lion's share of limited food. Bucks two and a half or more years in age usually are most dominant, followed in declining rank by prime-age does (those two and a half to eight and a half years old), old-age does, yearlings of both sexes, male fawns, and doe fawns. However, a deer's physical size and general health status will also greatly influence its competitive spirit and resultant success when fighting over access to limited food.

When crowded or challenged, dominant deer tend to hold their ground and retaliate, whereas subordinates are more inclined to avoid conflict. In crowded situations, as commonly occur at winter cuttings where deer are fed artificially, one deer may sometimes strike another from behind without warning. Deer with wounds and hair missing along their backs and sides — or, occasionally, one with a broken back — are probably victims of such action and indicative of intense social strife.

Wintering whitetails are remarkably adaptable animals, but by no means do they possess infallible ecological wisdom. Stressed animals in particular may at times unwisely sacrifice quality shelter for superior nutrition of sporadic occurrence, trade-offs that can result in dangerous wintering habits. A series of successive easy winters coupled with increased browse availability produced by logging or outright artificial feeding can perpetuate deer occupation of widely scattered, poorly sheltered sites. While some people may view such dispersion of deer on winter range as a favorable alternative to large concentrations of deer within core areas of traditional yards, these satellite herds sometimes suffer high and even complete mortality when faced with especially tough winters

Male whitetails shed their antlers at the conclusion of their annual breeding cycle when their testosterone levels decrease. Prior to casting its antlers, this buck shakes its head in an attempt to detach the loosening rack it has worn for the better part of the year. The buck may cast one antler at a time, sometimes up to a day or two apart, or both may be shed almost simultaneously, within minutes of one another.

and reduced food supplies. Weakened deer in small, widely scattered groups also become easy prey for predators.

Smaller groups of deer might lessen direct competition for food, but many social groups of deer congregating in a given area of good shelter provide certain valuable antipredation benefits. A large aggregation of deer will create a system of trails that can serve as escape routes when deer are chased by predators. Also, socially compatible deer that bed in groups provide greater sensory capability for detecting predators, which permits each deer to spend less time alert and more time feeding and ruminating, and an aggregation's quail-like scattering when confronted with danger tends to confuse predators as well. Predation thus also becomes much more selective because predators "test" a group of deer, then select as prey those that are slower, weaker, and more vulnerable.

Major predators of wintering whitetails include the timber wolf, mountain lion, coyote, bobcat, and domestic dog. Among these, the wolf and the mountain lion are by far the most efficient but also the least common. Today, wolves and white-tailed deer share range only in remote areas of northern Wisconsin, Michigan, Minnesota, and in southern

Canada. The ranges of mountain lions and whitetails overlap only in portions of the Rocky Mountains, the Southwest, and in isolated pockets in Florida.

Where wolves still occur in fair numbers, such as in northern Minnnesota and Canada, they can be effective predators of deer. In winter, a wolf pack will kill a deer every few days, but the pack's members tend to take a disproportionate number of deer that have some sort of abnormality, such as old deer afflicted with arthritis or fawns with low fat supplies. Adult bucks, relative to their availability, generally comprise a greater percentage of deer kills by wolves, indicating a sex-related vulnerability to wolf predation.

Bobcats kill some deer in winter but are more dependent on rabbits, hares, and other small mammals and birds for food. Bobcats reportedly hunt mostly at night, stalking deer in their beds. If successful in its stalk, the cat pounces on the deer's back, bites the deer's throat, and punctures its windpipe. The consensus among biologists, however, is that bobcat predation is usually not enough to seriously affect deer numbers.

Coyotes, although considered a more serious threat to newborn fawns, are also capable of killing adult deer that are weakened by malnutrition or hindered in their escape by deep snow. The chances of a coyote killing a healthy adult deer, however, seem poor at best. Most studies reveal that coyotes come upon deer quite by accident, do minimal stalking, and then give chase as the surprised prey flee. In the dense conifer cover typical of core yarding areas, the coyote's chase, successful or not, usually consists of a short "testing" dash toward the deer. As a result, coyotes more commonly bring down the smallest and weakest animals — those least likely to survive the winter.

There is considerable evidence indicating that the most serious four-footed predator of white-tailed deer is the domestic dog. Although deer-killing dogs are usually considered to be stray of feral, numerous well-kept house and yard pets are guilty of such action. Furthermore, dog owners are more apt to blame coyotes or other wild animals for preying on deer. Dogs are most perilous to young fawns, but they frequently kill adult deer, apparently for "sport," and their harassment of pregnant does and chasing of undernourished deer during late winter likely contributes to additional stress and death of some deer that might otherwise have survived.

The whitetail's impressive adaptations for winter survival diminish in value around mid-March, when, in response to increasing photoperiod, the animals' metabolism shifts back to a higher level. Thereafter, steadily increasing food demands render deer once again exceedingly sensitive to environmental stress factors. Depending on prevailing temperatures, snow depths, and rate of snow melt, deer sometimes experience extremely hazardous and exhausting travel conditions at spring break-up, making a bad situation even worse.

Death from malnutrition, a relatively common phenomenon in overpopulated deer wintering areas, is a pathetically slow process. But outright death from starvation only represents part of the problem. Among whitetails, most such mortality occurs in March and April, only after each animal has consumed much available browse, which results in rapid habitat deterioration and decreases an area's future capacity to support healthy deer. Thus, even the survivors are poorly served because fewer deer initially would have meant more available food resources per individual. Malnourished deer also become easy prey for predators, and those whitetails that are injured, diseased, heavily parasitized, or physically stressed may incur irreversible damage to the rumen lining and die, regardless of any subsequent improvement in food availability.

White-tailed deer carry the normal complement of relatively harmless external and internal parasites, including ticks, lice, fleas, liver flukes, tapeworms, round worms, and nasal bots. They also harbor the meningeal "brain" worm (a parasite that is readily transmitted and can be lethal to moose, pronghorn antelope, elk, and mountain sheep), with no ill effects. However, certain internal parasites may cause significant mortality among deer subjected to food shortage. Several types of stomach worms are especially widespread in deer and can be deadly when deer are overly abundant and malnourished.

Even deer experimentally fed unlimited amounts of nutritious pelletized feed restrict their food consumption and may lose from 10 to 15 percent of their body weight over winter. Thus, appreciable weight loss by whitetails during the winter season seems

This buck, having just cast its right antler, glances about warily as blood trickles down the side of its head from the antler's former point of attachment.
When found, freshly shed antlers are often seen on blood-spotted snow or forest litter.

A whitetail, a victim of disease and winter's stressful, demanding conditions, lies dead in a forest creek bottom. Over winter and into spring, as weather varied from freezes to thaws, the deer's remains became encased in ice until only the antlers remained visible on the floor of the ravine.

inevitable and natural, regardless of their diet.

Does and fawns that enter winter with maximum fat reserves can usually withstand upwards of 30 percent weight loss without dying. By comparison, as result of their strenuous rutting activity, adult bucks commonly enter winter already relatively lean, making them particularly vulnerable if winter weather is severe and food scarce. Fawns generally are the first to die, however, and regularly represent 70 percent or more of the overwinter mortality. But old deer are also highly susceptible to winter stress; few does in excess of 16 years old or bucks older than 12 years are likely to survive tough northern winters.

Obviously, extreme weather severity during January and February alone is not especially deadly for whitetails; that is when deer are geared-down physiologically and adjusted behaviorally to withstand great adversity. Instead, it's the prolonged winters of early onset or delayed break-up which overlap seasonal periods of high energy demand that can be so devastating.

Although thousands of northern whitetails may die during a severe winter, outright starvation represents only a small portion of that mortality. The effects of a severe winter are truly two-fold, as malnutrition among pregnant does during the latter third of gestation, in particular, contributes to poor fetal growth and, ultimately, to high infant mortality rates. Following a tough winter, newborn fawns hopelessly stunted by poor

These whitetail yearlings are entering winter in a healthy, fat condition. Given at least a sustenance diet and normal winter weather conditions, they can withstand the rigors of cold winds and food scarcity, but they may use all their fat reserves in doing so and enter spring at only 70 percent of their current weight.

nutrition die at an alarming rate. These hidden losses invariably far outnumber the more conspicuous winter starvation deaths.

Adequate food and cover in suitable locations are commodities vital to the overwinter survival of whitetails throughout their range in North America. Southern deer must find such essentials within the boundaries of their comparatively small year-round home range. The complexity and richness of that range in terms of whitetail food and cover availability — the area's carrying capacity — will determine the number of deer it can maintain in a healthy and vigorous condition.

In the South, biologists can, with fair precision, generally determine optimal deer numbers for any given area by conducting forage surveys or by closely monitoring such deer welfare indicators as reproduction, mortality, sex and age ratios, antler size, and average body weights. When deer numbers exceed an area's optimal level, habitat deterioration and subsequent shortages in food availability will adversely impact deer health and productivity, threatening their very survival. When deer density exceeds an area's favorable limit, some deer must die so that others may live, and the survivors will fare poorly.

Somewhat different circumstances prevail when determining favorable deer herd size in the North. There the main problem involves the whitetail's yarding habit, its critical need for winter shelter, and the absence of foods high in energy content. Annual differences in winter severity confound matters even more so, as any deer yard can logically support more deer during short, mild winters than during those of prolonged severity. No amount of high-quality cover will make up for an inadequate food supply, however, as even well-sheltered, initially fat deer will eventually succumb to prolonged malnutrition. Furthermore, because each deer yard supports animals from a specific segment of its surrounding area, with little overlap of deer from neighboring yards, a massive die-off of deer from a certain yard could cause a sparse deer population on its associated summering grounds for years to come, regardless of the capacity of that non-wintering habitat to support deer. Thus, the amount of good-quality winter food is the proverbial bottleneck that ultimately determines how many whitetails can survive the stressful northern winter, but calculating a given northern area's precise deer carrying capacity becomes a rather unavailing exercise because of the number of highly variable factors that may affect it from one year to the next.

Although the spatial requirements of white-tailed deer are poorly understood, our investigations at Cusino indicate that there are upper limits beyond which herd density becomes detrimental to herd welfare, regardless of food availability. We've found, for example, that once deer density in our enclosure herd surpassed 100 deer per square mile, young does bred later than normal and conceived fewer fawns, adult does produced proportionately fewer female fawns, newborn fawn mortality escalated among first-time mothers, body size decreased among young deer, and many yearling bucks grew short "spikes" instead of forked antlers even when the herd had ready access to favorable shelter and unlimited nutritious food. In other words, consequences solely of social stress due to crowding can impact the health and survival of deer just as effectively as poor nutrition.

Today, whitetails living in the near absence of effective natural predators are often their own worst enemy. An overabundance of deer in many sections of the country threatens the whitetail's healthful existence. If combined mortality from all causes, hunting included, fails to balance deer numbers with available food, cover, and spatial resources, then parasitism, disease, malnutrition, and social stress will interact to affect deer health, reproduction, and survival to the point of slowing and finally reversing a given population's size. Unfortunately, natural control mechanisms are slow to operate, wasteful of resources, result in severe damage to habitat, and invariably stabilize deer populations at unacceptably low levels. Sensible alternatives to natural regulation of whitetail populations include habitat improvement (designed to maximize deer range carrying capacity) in conjunction with strict herd control (accomplished through regulated deer harvesting by hunters). And in order to maintain healthy and thriving deer populations, a reasonable hunter-take of both sexes of deer not only becomes possible, today it is absolutely necessary in most regions of the country.

The white-tailed deer is opportunistic and an admirably adaptive and wily creature that possesses immense genetic plasticity. Such adaptiveness has permitted whitetails to invade and successfully occupy widely contrasting, sometimes seemingly hostile environments and to cope with, as a result of human-induced mortality, rather drastic changes in

their population densities and sex-age structures.

It should be emphasized, however, that human predation of deer differs markedly from that imposed on them by natural predators. Natural predators preponderantly kill the young, very old, and physically unfit deer, a process that ensures physical fitness within the herd, whereas American hunters prefer to take the very best, prime whitetail specimens. Antlered bucks, regardless of their age, are routinely harvested so intensively in many areas of the country that few survive the annual deer harvest. At the same time, because of the stigma associated with shooting a small deer, hunters shy away from cropping fawns, which occur in greatest abundance and are most vulnerable to winter stress. And ironically, excessive harvesting of antlered bucks in northern regions is accompanied by frequent and heavy overwinter mortality of malnourished fawns.

Research has shown that hunter-induced mortality (or the lack of it) among whitetails can seriously alter the animals' social environment and that it can impact, either favorably or unfavorably, deer reproductive performance — a situation which shouldn't be ignored in progressive management of deer herds. But many important questions regarding the welfare of white-tailed deer remain to be answered. Whether continuous intensive cropping of the "best" whitetail specimens contributes to serious social disruption and genetic degradation and is eventually detrimental to the healthful existence of whitetails, as some investigators suggest, has not been demonstrated to the satisfaction of most wildlife managers. Nonetheless, while researchers probe such intriguing questions to learn more about the whitetail's behavior and social requirements, certain actions could be taken. In order to more effectively control deer populations in some areas or to maximize the species' reproductive performance in others, for example, deer herd management strategies could become considerably more complex and sophisticated.

As unpopular as such change may be, the deer hunter of the future may be required to play a much more responsible predator role, for the good of the hunter, the non-hunter, and the hunted. The transition will no doubt be a slow and difficult one, and it will be totally impossible without the cooperation of knowledgeable, perceptive hunters and the full support of an enlightened and understanding non-hunting public.

A doe munches on a willow twig, sustenance that may or may not be enough to allow her and the fetuses she is carrying to survive to the end of winter, to another spring in whitetail country.

SELECTED REFERENCES

Atkeson, T.D., and R.L. Marchinton 1982. Forehead glands in white-tailed deer. J. Mammal. 63:613-617.

Atkeson, T.D., V.F. Nettles, R.L. Marchinton, and W.V. Branan. 1988. Nasal glands in Cervidae. J. Mammal. (in press).

Bahnak, B.R., J.C. Holland, L.J. Verme, and J.J. Ozoga. 1979. Seasonal and nutritional effects on serum nitrogen constituents in white-tailed deer. J. Wildl. Manage. 43:454-460.

Beasom, S.L. 1974. Relationships between predator removal and white-tailed deer net productivity. J. Wildl. Manage. 38:854-859.

Brown, B.A. 1974. Social organization in male groups of white-tailed deer. Pages 436-446 in V. Geist and F. Walther, eds. The behavior of ungulates and its relation to management. Int. Union Conserv. Nat. Pub. 24, Morges, Switzerland. IUCN. 940 pp.

Brown, R.D., ed. 1983. Antler development in Cervidae. Caesar Kleberg Wildl. Res. Inst., Kingsville, Texas, 480 pp.

Bubenik, A.B. 1972. North American moose management in light of European experiences. North Am. Moose Conf. Workshop 8:276-295.

Carroll, B.K., and D.L. Brown. 1977. Factors affecting neonatal fawn survival in south-central Texas. J. Wildl. Manage. 41:63-69.

Cook, R.S., M. White, D.O. Trainer, and W.C. Glazener. 1967. Radio-telemetry for fawn mortality studies. Wildl. Dis. Assoc. Bull. 3:160-165.

Cook, R.S., M. White, D.O. Trainer, and W.C. Glazener. 1971. Mortality of young white-tailed deer fawns in South Texas. J. Wildl. Manage. 35:47-56.

Garner, G.W., and J.A. Morrison. 1980. Observations of interspecific behavior between predators and white-tailed deer in southwestern Oklahoma. J. Mammal. 61:126-130.

Garner, G.W., J.A. Morrison, and J.C. Lewis. 1978. Mortality of white-tailed deer fawns in the Wichita Mountains, Oklahoma. Proc. Annu. Conf. Southeast. Assoc. Fish and Wildl. Agencies. 30:493-506.

Geist, V. 1974. On the relationship of social evolution and ecology in ungulates. Am. Zool. 14:206-220.

Goss, R.J. 1983. Deer antlers: regeneration, function, and evolution. Academic Press, NY. 316 pp.

Gruver, B.J., D.C. Guynn, Jr., and H.A. Jacobson. 1984. Simulated effects of harvest strategy on reproduction in white-tailed deer. J. Wildl. Manage. 48:535-541.

Halls, L.K., ed. 1984. White-tailed deer: ecology and management. Wildl. Manage. Inst., The Stackpole Co., Harrisburg, PA. 870 pp.

Haugen, A.O. 1975. Reproductive performance of white-tailed deer in Iowa. J. Mammal. 56:151-159.

Haugen, A.O., and D.W. Speake. 1958. Determining age of young fawn white-tailed deer. J. Wildl. Manage. 22:319-321.

Hawkins, R.E., and W.D. Klimstra. 1970. A preliminary study of the social organization of white-tailed deer. J. Wildl. Manage. 34:407-419.

Hawkins, R.E., W.D. Klimstra, and D.C. Autry. 1971. Dispersal of deer from Crab Orchard National Wildlife Refuge. J. Wildl. Manage. 35:216-220.

Hirth, D.H. 1977. Social Behavior of white-tailed deer in relation to habitat. Wildl. Monogr. 53. 55 pp.

Hoffman, R.A. and P.F. Robinson. 1966. Changes in some endocrine glands of white-tailed deer as affected by season, sex and age. J. Mammal. 47:266-280.

Hoskinson, R.L. and L.D. Mech. 1976. White-tailed deer migration and its role in wolf predation. J. Wildl. Manage. 40:429-441.

Huegel, C.N., R.B. Dahlgren, and H.L. Gladfelter. 1985. Mortality of white-tailed deer fawns in south-central Iowa. J. Wildl. Manage. 49:377-380.

Inglis, J.M., R.E. Hood, B.A. Brown, and C.A. DeYoung. 1979. Home range of white-tailed deer in Texas coastal prairie brushland. J. Mammal. 60:377-389.

Jackson, R.M., M. White, and F.F. Knowlton. 1972. Activity patterns of young white-tailed deer fawns in south Texas. Ecology 53:262-270.

Jacobsen, N.K. 1979. Alarm bradycardia in white-tailed deer fawns (Odocoileus virginianus). J. Mammal. 60:343-349.

Kammermeyer, K.E., and R.L. Marchinton. 1977. Seasonal change in circadian activity of radio-monitored deer. J. Wildl. Manage. 41:315-317.

Kile, T.L., and R.L. Marchinton. 1977. White-tailed deer rubs and scrapes: spatial, temporal and physical characteristics and social role. Am. Midl. Nat. 97:257-266.

Langaneau, E.E., Jr., and J.M. Lerg. 1976. The effects of winter nutritional stress on maternal and neonatal behavior in penned white-tailed deer. Appl. Anim. Ethology 2:207-223.

Larson, T.J., O.J. Rongstad, and F.W. Terbilcox. 1978. Movement and habitat use of white-tailed deer in southcentral Wisconsin. J. Wildl. Manage. 42:113-117.

Lent, P.C. 1974. Mother-infant relationships in ungulates. Pages 14-55 in V. Geist and F. Walther, eds. The behavior of ungulates and its relation to management. Int. Union Conserv. Nat. Publ. 24, Morges, Switzerland: IUCN. 940 pp.

Marchinton, R.L., and T.D. Atkeson. 1985. Plasticity of socio-spatial behavior of white-tailed deer and the concept of faculative territoriality. Internat. Conf. Biology of Deer Production. Dunedin, New Zealand. pp. 375-377.

McCullough, D.R. 1979. The George Reserve deer herd. Univ. Michigan Press, Ann Arbor. 271 pp.

Michael, E.D. 1964. Birth of white-tailed deer fawns. J. Wildl. Manage. 28:171-173.

Michael, E.D. 1965. Movements of white-tailed deer on the Welder Wildlife Refuge. J. Wildl. Manage. 29:44-52.

Miller, K.V., K.E. Kammermeyer, R.L. Marchinton, and B. Moser. 1987. Population and habitat influences on antler rubbing by white-tailed deer. J. Wildl. Manage. 51:62-66.

Miller, K.V., R.L. Marchinton, and W.M. Knox. White-tailed deer signposts and their role as a source of priming pheromones: a hypothesis. Pres. XVII Congress of the International Union of Game Biologists, Krakow, Poland, Aug. 23-29, 1987. (in press).

Moen, A.N. 1968. Energy balance of white-tailed deer in winter. Trans. N. Am. Wildl. and Natur. Resour. Conf. 33:224-236.

Moen, A.N. 1968. Energy exchange of white-tailed deer, western Minnesota. Ecology 49:676-682.

Moen, A.N. 1976. Energy conservation by white-tailed deer in the winter. Ecology 57:192-198.

Moore, W.G., and R.L. Marchinton. 1974. Marking behavior and its social function in white-tailed deer. in The behavior of ungulates and its relation to management, V. Geist and F.R. Walther, eds., pp. 447-456. Int. Union Conserv. Nat. Publ. 24, Morges, Switzerland: IUCN 940 pp.

Nelson, M.E. 1979. Home range location of white-tailed deer. USDA For. Serv. Pap. NC-173. Nor. Cent. For. Expt. Sta., St. Paul, MN. 10 pp.

Nelson, M.E., and L.D. Mech. 1981. Deer social organization and wolf predation in northeastern Minnesota. Wildl. Monogr. 77. 53 pp.

Nelson, M.E. and L.D. Mech. 1986. Mortality of white-tailed deer in northeastern Minnesota. J. Wildl. Manage. 50:691-701.

Nielsen, D.G., M.J. Dunlap, and K.V. Miller. 1982. Pre-rut rubbing by white-tailed bucks: nursery damage, social role, and management options. Wildl. Soc. Bull. 10:341-348.

Nixon, C.M. 1971. Productivity of white-tailed deer in Ohio. Ohio J. Sci. 71:217-225.

Ozoga, J.J. 1968. Variations in microclimate in a conifer swamp deeryard in northern Michigan. J. Wildl. Manage. 32:574-585.

_____ 1987. Maximum fecundity in supplementally fed northern Michigan white-tailed deer. J. Mammal. 36:878-879.

_____ 1988. Incidence of "infant" antlers among supplementally fed white-tailed deer. J. Mammal. (in press).

_____, and L.W. Gysel. 1972. Response of white-tailed deer to winter weather. J. Wildl. Manage. 36:892-896.

_____, and E.M. Harger. 1966. Winter activities and feeding habits of northern Michigan coyotes. J. Wildl. Manage. 30:809-818.

_____, and L.J. Verme. 1970. Winter feeding patterns of penned white-tailed deer. J. Wildl. Manage. 34:431-439.

_____, and L.J. Verme. 1975. Activity patterns of white-tailed deer during esterus. J. Wildl. Manage. 39:679-683.

_____, and L.J. Verme. 1982. Physical and reproductive characteristics of a supplementally fed white-tailed deer herd. J. Wildl. Manage. 46:281-301.

_____, and L.J. Verme. 1982. Predation by black bears on newborn white-tailed deer. J. Mammal. 63:695-696.

_____, and L.J. Verme. 1984. Effects of family-bond deprivation on reproductive performance in female white-tailed deer. J. Wildl. Manage. 48:1326-1334.

_____, and L.J. Verme. 1985. Comparative breeding behavior and performance of yearlings vs. prime-age white-tailed bucks. J. Wildl. Manage. 49:364-372.

_____, and L.J. Verme. 1985. Determining fetuses age in live white-tailed does by x-ray. J. Wildl. Manage. 49:374-376.

_____, and L.J. Verme. 1986. Initial and subsequent maternal success of white-tailed deer. J. Wildl. Manage. 50:122-124.

_____, and L.J. Verme. 1986. Relation of maternal age to fawn-rearing success of white-tailed deer. J. Wildl. Manage. 50:480-486.

_____, L.J. Verme, and S.C. Bienz. 1982. Parturition behavior and territoriality in white-tailed deer: impact on neonatal mortality. J. Wildl. Manage. 46:1-11.

_____, C.S. Bienz, and L.J. Verme. 1982. Red fox feeding habits in relation to fawn mortality. J. Wildl. Manage. 46:242-243.

Peterle, T.J. 1975. Deer sociobiology. Wildl. Soc. Bull. 3:82-83.

Plotka, E.D., U.S. Seal, L.J. Verme, and J.J. Ozoga. 1983. The adrenal gland in white-tailed deer: a significant source of progesterone. J. Wildl. Manage. 47:38-44.

Richardson, L.W., H.A. Jacobson, R.J. Muncy, and C.J. Perkins. 1983. Acoustics of white-tailed deer (*Odocoileus virginianus*). J. Mammal. 64:245-252.

Rongstad, O.J., and J.R. Tester. 1969. Movements and habitat use of white-tailed deer in Minnesota. J. Wildl. Manage. 33:366-379.

Sage, R.W., Jr., W.C. Tierson, G.F. Mattfeld, and D.F. Behrend. 1983. White-tailed deer visibility and behavior along forest roads. J. Wildl. Manage. 47:940-953.

Sawyer, T.G., R.L. Marchinton, and C.W. Berisford. 1982. Scraping behavior in female white-tailed deer. J. Mammal. 63:696-697.

Seal, U.D., L.J. Verme, J.J. Ozoga, and E.D. Plotka. 1983. Metabolic and endocrine responses of white-tailed deer to increasing population density. J. Wildl. Manage. 47:451-462.

Short, H.L. 1964. Postnatal stomach development of white-tailed deer. J. Wildl. Manage. 28:445-458.

Silver, H., N.F. Colovos, J.B. Holter, and H.H. Hayes. 1969. Fasting metabolism of white-tailed deer. J. Wildl. Manage. 33:490-498.

Sparrowe, R.D., and P.F. Springer. 1970. Seasonal activity patterns of white-tailed deer in eastern South Dakota. J. Wildl. Manage. 34:420-431.

Thomas, J.W., R.M. Robinson, and R.G. Marburger. 1965. Social behavior in a white-tailed deer herd containing hypogonadal males. J. Mammal. 46:314-327.

Tierson, W.C., G.F. Mattfeld, R.W. Sage, Jr., and D.F. Behrend. 1985. Seasonal movements and home ranges of white-tailed deer in the Adirondacks. J. Wildl. Manage. 49:760-769.

Townsend, T.W., and E.D. Bailey. 1975. Parturitional, early maternal, and neonatal behavior in penned white-tailed deer. J. Mammal. 56:347-362.

Townsend, T.W., and E.D. Bailey. 1981. Effects of age, sex, and weight social rank in penned white-tailed deer. Am. Midl. Nat. 106:92-101.

Verme, L.J. 1962. Mortality of white-tailed deer fawns in relation to nutrition. Proc. Nat. White-tailed Deer Symp. 1:15-38.

_____ 1963. Effect of nutrition on growth of white-tailed deer fawns. Trans. N. Amer. Wildl. and Natur. Resour. Conf. 28:431-443.

_____ 1965. Reproduction studies on penned white-tailed deer. J. Wildl. Manage. 29:74-79.

_____ 1968. An index of winter severity for northern deer. J. Wildl. Manage. 32:566-574.

_____ 1969. Reproductive patterns of white-tailed deer related to nutritional plane. J. Wildl. Manage. 33:881-887.

_____ 1973. Movements of white-tailed deer in Upper Michigan. J. Wildl. Manage. 37:545-552.

_____ 1977. Assessment of natal mortality in Upper Michigan. J. Wildl. Manage. 41:700-708.

_____ 1983. Sex ratio variations in *Odocoileus*: a critical review. J. Wildl. Manage. 47:573-582.

_____, and W.F. Johnston. 1985. Regeneration of northern white cedar deeryards in Upper Michigan. J. Wildl. Manage. 50:307-313.

_____, and J.J. Ozoga. 1971. Influence of weather on white-tailed deer in Upper Michigan. *In* Proc. snow and ice in relation to wildlife and recreation symp., ed. A.O. Haugen, pp. 16-28. Ames: Iowa Cooperative Wildlife Research Unit, Iowa State University. 280 pp.

_____, and J.J. Ozoga. 1980. Influence of protein-energy intake on deer fawns in autumn. J. Wildl. Manage. 44:305-314.

_____, and J.J. Ozoga. 1980. Effect of diet on growth and lipogenesis in deer fawns. J. Wildl. Manage. 44:315-324.

_____, and J.J. Ozoga. 1981. Sex ratio of white-tailed deer and the estrus cycle. J. Wildl. Manage. 45:710-715.

_____, and J.J. Ozoga. 1987. Relationships of photoperiod to puberty in doe white-tailed deer. J. Mammal. 68:107-110.

_____, J.J. Ozoga, and J.T. Nellist. 1987. Induced early estrus in penned white-tailed deer. J. Wildl. Manage. 51:54-56.

White, M., F.F. Knowlton, and W.C. Glazener. 1972. Effects of dam-newborn fawn behavior on capture and mortality. J. Wildl. Manage. 36:897-906.

Woodson, D.L., E.T. Reed, R.L. Downing, and B.S. McGinnes. 1980. Effects of fall orphaning on white-tailed deer fawns and yearlings. J. Wildl. Manage. 44:249-252.

Woolf, A., and J.D. Harder. 1979. Population dynamics of a captive white-tailed deer herd with emphasis on reproduction and mortality. Wildl. Monogr. 67. 53 pp.

Zagata, M.D., and A.O. Haugen. 1974. Influence of light and weather on observability of Iowa deer. J. Wildl. Manage. 38:220-228.

_____, and A.N. Moen. 1974. Antler shedding by white-tailed deer in the Midwest. J. Mammal. 55:656-659.